When The
Elephant
Laughed

Charleston, SC
www.PalmettoPublishing.com

When The Elephant Laughed
Copyright © 2022 by Reverend Dave Clements

First Edition

Paperback ISBN: 979-8-88590-690-6
eBook ISBN: 979-8-88590-691-3

Reverend Dave Clements

When The Elephant Laughed

TABLE OF CONTENTS

DEDICATION

I dedicate this book to Jerry, my life partner, for his constant support and encouragement.

To Michael, my friend and editor, who without his watchful eye and inspiration the details of the book would not have happened. To the members of the Unitarian Church in Cape Town, South Africa who gave me the opportunity to lead, learn and be taught by them.

FOREWORD

It has been my pleasure to know Reverend Dave Clements since 1998. We met in one of the most unusual places — on a busy subway platform in San Francisco, at rush hour. I had noticed him for several weeks leading up to our chance encounter. There was just something about Dave that caught my eye from the start — his presence, the way he carried himself, and a glimmer in his eye. On the evening of our formal introduction, it had been pouring down rain and there was a major system delay on MUNI, San Francisco's rapid transit system.

Somehow, we ended up standing right next to each other on the platform, both tired, frustrated, and with crowds of people filling the station behind us. In a moment of pure serendipity, Dave turned toward me and said, "Hi, my name is Dave, would you like to share a cab?" Without hesitation I said, "Boy would I", and we were off. We hailed a cab and much to my surprise, Dave told the driver, "48th and Lawton". "What?", I said out loud. "I'm at 43rd and Irving. We are neighbors!" Being as we lived at the far end of the city, near Ocean Beach, the cab ride took a good 30 minutes. The conversation was effortless. Even though I had just met Dave, I felt I had known him all my life. He was just that easy to talk to and I knew we would become fast friends.

In fact, we became best friends in the years that followed. One of the many highlights of my friendship with Dave was training for and completing the California AIDS Ride together in 1999. This entailed riding our bikes from San Francisco to Los Angeles, a journey of over 500 miles. Dave and I completed that ride together on a hot June day in Los Angeles, riding triumphantly over the finish line. The entire trip, from start to finish, was a bonding experience and gave us both such a sense of accomplishment and satisfaction. Completing this seemingly impossible challenge together, I knew I had a friend for life in Dave.

Dave is such a good friend, in fact, that when a vacant apartment became available in his building, he recommended me to the landlord, and I got the apartment. Over the next several years we grew even closer as friends and confidantes. I could tell Dave anything and he was always so supportive of me. A best friend in every sense of the word. Dave also served as a mentor to me and the big brother I never had. I hit the friendship jackpot by meeting Dave years earlier on that subway platform.

Like longstanding friendships, we have been through a lot together. Through relationship changes, career changes, and changes in residence, we've always been there for each other. Even though he moved to the Midwest over 15 years ago to pursue new career opportunities, we've never been closer. I always look forward to picking up the phone to call Dave or receiving a call from him; we easily pick up right where we left off. Whenever we do get to see each other in person, it's always a happy reunion.

One day, on one such phone call, Dave told me he had big news. "I've decided to go to ministry school in Chicago to become ordained in the Unitarian church", he said excitedly. Without missing a beat, I said "of course, you are!" This news did not surprise me one bit. I've always known Dave to pursue great things with great determination; I knew Dave would make a great minister because he has a way of bringing people together and is a natural-born leader.

In what seemed like a flash of the eye, one day he began his studies, and the next day I was on a plane flying to Cleveland to witness his ordination. This was in the Fall of 2017, and I was never prouder for his amazing achievement.

With his studies behind him, he then began his search for interim ministerial positions, not just in the Cleveland area, his home base, but he bravely cast a wide net searching across the United States. He diligently did his homework, spending lots of time researching different cities and different congregations. He had many great interviews and met a lot of great people. And yet, strangely, the job offers weren't coming in. I told him, "They're all fools for not hiring you." But Dave was persistent and patient with the process. He said something to the effect of, "good things come to those who wait."

So, he waited and waited and waited some more until one day my phone rang. It was Dave. He said, "you'll never guess what". "What?", I asked. "I just got off a Zoom call with the Unitarian Church in Cape Town, South Africa, and they are interested in bringing me on as their interim minister." "Wow", I exclaimed. "This is fantastic news and what an intriguing opportunity."

"I thought I was casting a wide net when considering opportunities in the U.S., but I didn't realize my net would encompass South Africa!", Dave replied.

I thought long and carefully for a moment before saying three simple words to Dave, "Go for it!" Knowing Dave for as long as I have, I knew in my heart at that moment that he would indeed go for it.

I'll let Dave tell the rest of the story from here, the year he spent as the interim minister in Cape Town, South Africa. In this book, you will learn all about his travel and adventures and quite a bit of history of South Africa along the way. Enjoy!

Michael Henley
Oakland, California

March 24, 2022

PROLOGUE

When you hear the words South Africa what comes to your mind? Most of us have heard about Nelson Mandela and his fight for freedom, or perhaps in your education you studied and learned about apartheid. Others may have heard of the term "Rainbow Nation" and not known that it originated in South Africa. It was first coined by Archbishop Desmond Tutu to describe post-apartheid South Africa after its first democratic election in 1994. The description of South Africa being a Rainbow Nation is on display each day with its mixtures of cultures and languages.

Did you know that South Africa is also a land of natural wonders? Over ten percent of the world's bird, fish, and plant species, as well as 6% of mammal and reptile species can be found there. Lions, elephants, and giraffes are plentiful in South Africa and South Africa has some of the world's best game preserves.

South Africa is the largest producer of macadamia nuts in the world. The country is five times the size of Japan and three times the size of Texas. South Africa is a treasure trove for archaeologists and paleontologists as it has produced some of the world's oldest and most valuable fossils to date. About a fifth of the world's gold hails from the mines of South Africa.

South Africa boasts 90% of the platinum metals on earth. Mossel Bay, which is in the Western Cape and along the beautiful Garden Route, has the second-most moderate climate of any other city or country in the world. Some of the most exciting sporting events that have been hosted in South Africa include the 1995 Rugby World Cup, 2003 Cricket World Cup, 2005 and 2006 Women's World Cup of Golf, 2006 Inaugural A1 GP World Cup of Motorsport, 2009 IPL Cricket, and the 2010 FIFA World Cup.

South Africa has 80% of the rail infrastructure of Africa. This country is home to the longest wine route in the world, the Cape Route 62, which is about 1,000 kilometers long and beautifully scenic.

Bloukrans Bridge is the highest commercial bungy jump in the world and is situated along the Garden Route. It is an impressive 216 meters high. Rooibos tea has become a worldwide favorite for its fresh taste and excellent health properties. It is only grown in a small region (in the Cederberg) of South Africa and is exported in massive quantities from there.

The South African coast boasts more than 2,000 shipwrecks. There are about 900 different avian species in South Africa, which represents around 10% of the bird species of the world. The magnificent Tugela Falls are the second highest on the globe, measuring some 850 meters (or 2,789 feet).

In Cape Town it is believed that the iconic Table Mountain is one of the oldest mountains in the world. Table Mountain is approximately 260 million years old; it is also home to thousands of species of plant life, including species unique to the Cape Floral Region. The glorious mountain is one of the world's Seven New Natural Wonders.

Did you know that another country lies within the borders of South Africa? The Kingdom of Lesotho is a sovereign state that is located in the Drakensberg Mountain area. The mountainous country has been nicknamed "the Kingdom in the Sky" thanks to the magnificent scenery and landscapes!

Most people don't know that a lot of things were invented in South Africa. Take the CAT scan, for instance, as well as the heart transplant, Silly Putty, and Q20 (the leading multi-purpose lubricant that protects against corrosion, stops rust, lubricates sticky mechanisms, and displaces moisture from electrical systems) to name a few. Having a look at South African inventions is bound to surprise you!

South Africa is a diverse, enticing, and intriguing country. Having the opportunity to live and work in South Africa as a Unitarian minister, I gained an appreciation for its diversity, its enticing beauty, and its intriguing history. The stories collected in this book were all taken from my daily journal.

South Africa has 11 official languages. Living and working in South Africa provided me with an opportunity to learn about the effects of apartheid on the daily lives of the people. Learning about the townships and their history provided me with an appreciation and understanding of community.

Working with interfaith religious leaders demonstrated to me what can be accomplished when people can come together around a central issue or purpose. Visiting historical sites allowed me to connect with the historical stories and gain a greater understanding of the sacrifices that these early elders made.

As you read through the chapters, it is my hope that you gain an understanding of the culture, the people, and the land that is called South Africa. Cape Town, South Africa is an incredible destination that draws people from all over the world to visit.

CHAPTER ONE:

ENTERING IN

Cape Town, South Africa is not a quick destination to reach by plane. Traveling from the United States can take anywhere from 28 to 35 hours. Not only is it a great distance from the USA it is also located in the Southern Hemisphere, half a world away. When we are experiencing summer here in the USA, they are experiencing winter. My journey to Cape Town, South Africa began in Cleveland, Ohio just before the start of winter. My excitement was building at the thought of leaving behind yet another cold, snowy winter bound for the sun-drenched shores of Cape Town, South Africa!

As luck would have it, I convinced my partner Jerry to accompany me for a few weeks to help me settle into my new surroundings. He was eager to escape winter in Cleveland. It was Jerry who had encouraged me to take advantage of this once in a lifetime opportunity to be hired by a Unitarian Congregation in Cape Town, South Africa. I am not sure who was more excited that day as we boarded our plane for Amsterdam and then onto Cape Town, South Africa, him, or me?

We boarded our plane to South Africa, full of excitement, great anticipation, and some anxiety. The journey had begun! Many thoughts started to swirl through my head. What will it be like? Will I fit in? What lessons will I learn? Even though I couldn't possibly know the answers to these questions, I knew that I was about to begin a journey that would be life changing.

Our flight left on time from Detroit to Amsterdam. Time passed quickly and as I was awakening from a restless night's sleep we were already landing in Amsterdam. We departed our plane and quickly realized that our flight to Cape Town was on the other side of the Amsterdam airport. About two hours before departure, we started our walk to the other side of the terminal.

During the long walk, I couldn't help but hear voices around us speaking in a variety of languages. I quickly realized that we were no longer in the USA. I stopped for a moment to take in the scene and watched as different cultures, ethnic nationalities, and personalities all passed by. For one moment it was as if the United Nations was passing us by. It was exciting and inspiring to observe this beautiful parade of humanity before my eyes. I had traveled before outside of the United States as a teenager, but it had been several years since I had traveled outside of the US. I felt as if I were standing inside of a movie set; I was a casual observer, like an extra, yet I also felt like part of the action.

I kept looking for someone who sounded and looked like me and yet everywhere I looked I came across people who were different then me in their language, dress, and culture. For a moment I longed for something familiar. Then suddenly, there in a store window at the Amsterdam Airport, I saw it. High up on the shelf was a small American Flag and a small statue of our US Capital. It brought me back to a reality that I was an American and that the eyes of the world might from time to time be on me as an example of what

America stands for. A warm feeling came over me with a real since of pride to be an American. Jerry and I picked up our pace.

What seemed like a long walk we arrived at our gate. We had a brief hour before boarding would begin. Sitting in the waiting area I listened and observed. In one area German was the language of choice. I knew it was German because of the sound of the vowels. The German alphabet includes the three standard vowel sounds for the letters a (ah), o (oh) and u (ooh), but when these letters are combined with the Umlaut as ä, ö, and ü, their pronunciation changes.

Behind us a couple were conversing in French and to the side of us were two people of color who appeared to be engaged in a deep conversation in an African dialect. African dialects are often referred to as click languages. These African dialects have very distinctive sounds, clicks are articulated in the mouth by a suction mechanism that produces either a sharp popping or smacking sound between the tongue and the roof of the mouth or a sucking sound between the lips (the kiss click) or teeth or at the side of the mouth. I recognized the click sound as being African and a smile came to my face as I visualized having many conversations with South Africans. In South Africa most South Africans speak three languages: Afrikaans, English and their native African language, which for most is ether Khoisan or Zulu.

My mind raced and for a moment I sat there feeling very much alone but quickly realized that I wasn't completely alone — my partner Jerry was there sitting right beside me. I looked at him and we both smiled, as if to say, "I'm glad you're here." Then I was struck with that brief thought, "I wonder if this is what individuals experience when they come to America for the first time?" They must long for someone, anyone who looks like them, whom they can relate to and feel safe being around.

A short time later we began boarding our flight to Cape Town. It was 10:30 am, Christmas Eve Day and within 12 hours we would be landing in South Africa. I was amazed that on the 24th of December so many people from around the world were traveling to this destination. Our flight was full; the flight attendants were busy attending to the various needs of our fellow passengers as each one tried to find their seat and put their luggage in the overhead compartment.

Then it happened. I heard the airplane door close. The sign appeared to fasten your seat belt. Jerry and I found our way to our seats, and I was struck with the thought. "This was it – "There's no turning back now." The jet engines roared and then the captains voice was heard as he welcomed all of us First in English, German and finally French. I sat back and realized that my new adventure and journey were only just beginning.

This was my first time traveling for 12 hours on a plane. It was a long journey and the hours provided me with time to stop and consider just what I was getting myself into. When I had made the decision to enter the ministry years before, I had thought about serving congregations in different parts of the US and Canada, but International Ministry had never crossed my mind. When the opportunity presented itself, my partner Jerry immediately encouraged me to apply.

Now I was on a path to begin an international ministry experience. I felt a certain amount of fear and trepidation but also confidence in being a newly ordained minister. I told myself out loud, "I got this." The fear and trepidation didn't go away buy I did feel a degree of calmness. In that moment I surrendered and felt that life lessons were already unfolding and would continue to unfold all around me.

It was 10:30pm Christmas day and we had landed in Cape Town, South Africa. As the plane moved toward our departure gate an excitement filled my soul. I couldn't imagine what would lie in store, but I felt ready to begin this new phase of my life. We sailed through customs, found our luggage, and looked for a sign, any sign of welcome from those members of the Unitarian church who had ventured out to meet us and take us to our hotel.

There in a far-off corner and quickly headed our way were our greeters, carrying a hand lettered sign, which read: "Welcome Rev. Dave and Jerry to South Africa!" We met our greeters and made our way to their cars. I almost fell over when our driver drove up and got out of the right side of the car. Wow! I knew that South Africans drove on the other side of the road but hadn't stopped to think that to do that would require the steering wheel to be on the right side of the car.

What seemed like well over an hour but most likely was less then 20 minutes, we arrived in the heart of Cape Town at our Airbnb. Our newfound Unitarian friends helped us to unload and wished us all the best and went on their way. We planned to meet up in a few days, but for now we were on our own.

Sleep came easy and I was awoken by what sounded like pipes clanging and voices yelling. I made my way to the balcony, flung open the sliding glass door and observed a busy scene five floors below me out on the plaza. My eyes focused and realized that the individuals were constructing a series of connecting stalls where they could display their hand made goods. It was amazing to see this span of humanity so engaged in the early morning building something that would serve as a backdrop for 12 hours for the day that was only just beginning.

My partner awoke and we descended from our safe cocoon and ventured out into a world where we had no idea what to expect. In no time we were quickly educated concerning the open-air market that surrounded us both. I learned that each day at 6:30am the vendors would arrive with their merchandise and would work at selling and trading them for the next 12 hours! This was their daily routine come rain or shine.

I had been to many swaps meets, garage sales and estate transactions over the years, but this unique open-air market was an eclectic mix of all these. Just about anything that was African made we could find on sale. As we meandered from trader to trader each one assured us that their merchandise was the best, one of a kind, and only on sale for today. Talk about a tough sell! There was so much to see, feel, and simply observe that it was overwhelming.

It was the day after Christmas and around 9:30 in the morning. Jerry and I were hungry and quickly looking for a place to grab some food. On the square was a hotel. We made our way there and found that the restaurant was open and serving breakfast. We were greeted and escorted to a table in the middle of a large room. A server appeared and greeted us warmly and offered her suggestions as to what she thought we might enjoy.

I quickly learned that a classic breakfast in Cape Town features eggs, slices of broiled tomato, Canadian-style bacon, and toast or pastries. Fresh fruit, granola and yogurt is also a common choice. A real delicacy is buttermilk rusks, which are best eaten after dipping for a few seconds in your morning coffee.

We were trying to blend in, but it was soon apparent to everyone that we were two white Americans who had arrived in Cape Town, South Africa. Our server asked us where we were from and what brought us to South Africa and to Cape Town. I shared that I was the Interim Minister for the Cape Town Unitarian Church. Much to my surprise she shared that she had attended services there and that one of her best friends was a member of the Cape Town congregation. What a small world! Jerry and I were both tired and adjusting to a new time zone, a new country, and a new place. Celine, our server, had just made our adjustment that much easier.

I learned Celine was a native of South Africa and was part of the Khoisan tribe. (Note: Racial groups in South Africa have a variety of origins. The racial categories introduced by Apartheid remain ingrained in South African society with South Africans continuing to classify themselves, and each other, as belonging to one of the four defined race groups; Black, Whites, Coloureds and Indians).

That day I had made a new friend and, in the months, ahead I would spend many more meals and sharing my current experiences with Celine. I had been in Cape Town for only 12 hours yet had connected with a person in a heart-to-heart manner; I just knew that Celine was a great example of the love and peaceful spirit of the South Africans.

Breakfast arrived, which for me consisted of scrambled eggs, South African sausage, and bacon. Jerry had his usual oatmeal with lots of milk. The most delightful surprise came in the form of a cappuccino that I had ordered. It hit my lips with a smack followed by a myriad of flavors. Celine brought some warm milk to go with the hot beverage. That morning I had my first taste of South African coffee, which for me was like no other coffee. It was out of this world. The flavors exploded in my mouth as if they were a rushing spring brook flowing over my tongue.

When the bill arrived, it showed that we owed 300 Rand for breakfast; we both gasped! We were thinking in US dollars, not Rands, which is the South African currency. Jerry did the conversion and the cost of our breakfast seemed perfectly reasonable, just $20 American dollars.

For the rest of the day, Jerry and I wandered leisurely throughout the open market — observing and taking in the place, soaking in the sights and sounds, the people, and the culture I would call home for the next year. The market was amazing; it was like walking through a world market store here in the states but with three times the merchandise. I quickly learned that market shopping is big in Cape Town. Locals love to spend summer evenings and weekends browsing the stalls, selling everything from curios to clothes, to delectable food and drinks.

As Jerry and I made our way back to our villa after a very full day, I realized that the first 48 hours had been a memorable experience and I couldn't help but wonder what new adventures, experiences, sights, and sounds lie in store for me to discover. What new cultural experiences would I encounter and what life lessons would I learn?

CHAPTER TWO:
MEETING THE CONGREGATION

One of the most exciting and yet very challenging times is when a minister meets the members of his congregation for the very first time. I had spoken to many of them by way of Zoom but now I would have the opportunity to meet them face to face. Many thoughts flooded through my mind that Sunday morning. "What would they be like, what would they think of me, what are they expecting?" These and many more thoughts raced through my mind in a rapid succession like a quickly moving kaleidoscope.

Jerry and I arrived at the church a full hour before services were to begin, just to be safe, and found the church entirely locked up. Immediately, anxious thoughts ran through my head: "Did we miss something", "did we have the right place", "right time, etc.?" No sooner had we started to walk away when my phone vibrated to indicate that a text message had just arrived. I read the message and was told that Shelly, the President of the Council, would be there shortly and to meet her at the Ground Art Café, a coffee shop just around the corner from the Unitarian Church.

Jerry and I made our way to cafe, which offered a combination of the artistic endeavors of Barista, Chef and Art Curator. I had read about the place in a tour brochure, and they stated that it was one of Cape Town's best coffee houses.

I ordered a cappuccino while Jerry selected an exotic passion fruit mango juice from a local Cape Town maker called Granor Passi. Shelly soon arrived and explained to me how the service would unfold. I was informed that after the offering I would be introduced and then be expected to share with the assembled members the thoughts, hopes and dreams that were on my heart. The three of us paid for our coffees and other items and made our way around the corner to the church.

The Unitarian Church was celebrating its 150th year and had been in their present building all but the first four years of their existence. The building had been a warehouse made from dusty old brown brick and looked old. Across the top of the building in bold letters were engraved into the stone: **The Free Church**. I walked up to the building and stopped and observed it up close. A feeling of awe and wonderment filled my being. I wondered about those who had gathered in this building over the years and the lives that they lived. I wondered about the leaders, both ministers and lay, who had guided, directed, and kept the congregation together. With humility I stopped and took a short breath. I would be making another mark on the rich history of this congregation. I wondered what challenges and experiences awaited me.

I took three steps and entered the building. I immediately felt a sense of peace and comfort come over me. I knew I was standing in a place where lives had been changed, where comfort had been offered and where people from all cultures and ethnic backgrounds had come together as a faith community. I was overcome with emotion as I realized the significance of my call and the opportunity to serve this congregation.

The building was not large but as I stood there for the first time that morning, I felt the presence of those who had served and of those members who understood what it means to be concerned for the worth and dignity of all people. I made my way to a seat a few rows from the pulpit and sat down. The place quickly filled, and my moment of reveal had begun. I don't remember much that transpired that morning, but I do recall my name been announced and being asked to make my way to the pulpit and address the congregation.

When I looked out, I saw the faces of many cultures, backgrounds, and nationalities. I was the minority in the room — a new feeling and experience for me. I was also one of very few Americans that were there that day. My mind quickly searched for words and somehow I found them. Much of what I said that day I don't remember but I do remember telling the congregants that starting that day I was inviting each of them to join me on this journey of discovery. I shared with them my excitement of being called and pledged that I would not disappoint them. Much after that is all a blur except for my closing words which were all about the importance of community and that we were and always will be a community of faith that offers a place of comfort, a place of peace, and a place of being. After I finished speaking, I sat down and felt proud that my South African ministry had begun.

CHAPTER THREE:
THE CENTRAL TASK

The central task of a religious community is to unveil the bonds that bind each of us to all. There is a connectedness, a relationship discovered amid the particulars of our own lives and the lives of others. Once felt, it inspires us to act, to stand up to let our voices be heard against the injustices in our community and world. It is the church that assures us that we are not struggling for justice on our own, but as members of a larger community. The religious community is essential, for alone our vision is too narrow to see all that must be seen, and our strength too limited to do all that must be done. Together, our vision widens, and our strength is renewed. — Rev. Mark Morrison Reed[1]

---

[1]The Central Task of the Religious Community" by Mark Morrison Reed; Tuesday November 26, 2013 18:40 +0

Through the years I had become familiar with many of the challenges of living and working in the various cities and communities of America. One of the challenges of living and serving in a foreign country is the loss of connection with the familiarity of friends, places, events, and American customs. I had spent all my adult life living and working in the United States and had developed deep friendships and rich relationships. Now I was called upon to forge a new path among an entirely new culture in a new land.

I had lived and worked in downtown Detroit, Michigan. While there, I had experienced what it was like to walk in an area of town where the color of my skin was an exception and not the norm. I had embraced that experience and knew that I could choose to avoid those parts of the city and gather in those areas where my whiteness was the custom or choose to be a part of the community. I choose to be a part of the community. I shopped at their stores, ate at their restaurants, and walked in their neighborhoods.

One thing that I came to understand, while living in downtown Detroit, was the many injustices that people of color faced in that city and the surrounding metro areas. While American society purports to be open and egalitarian, or all about equal opportunity, such everyday discriminations leave black people deeply doubtful. Among their own communities, black people affirm and reaffirm these central lessons and, out of a sense of duty, try to pass them along to others they care about, and especially to their children.

My experience of living and working in a city where I was in the minority gave me some sense of what it is like to not look like everyone else. As I look back on the experience of living in downtown Detroit, I can see how that experience prepared me for living and working in Cape Town, South Africa.

For the first month of my time in South Africa my partner Jerry was with me. I knew I was charting through new waters, but I always had Jerry right there by my side to guide me and support me. Eventually the time came when Jerry left to go back to our home and friends in the United States. So now it was now up to me to venture down this new path and journey that was opening before me. Friends, family, and relationships with ministry colleagues all became more important as I navigated this new experience.

Early one morning while studying I came across the African fable about an elephant in the room. In 1814 Ivan Andreevich wrote a fable entitled, "The Inquisitive Man."[2]

The fable tells the story of a man who goes to a museum and notices all sorts of tiny things but fails to notice the elephant in the room. When he comes out of the museum one of his colleagues asks him what he thought of the museum. The man goes on and on about all the tiny things he saw in the museum. The colleague asks him if he noticed the large elephant that was in the room. The man responds, "No, I didn't notice the elephant in the room."

From this simple story comes the expression the elephant in the room, which refers to "a big issue that we are aware of, but which is being ignored because everybody finds discussion about it uncomfortable." The rationale behind the idiom is that an elephant in a room would be impossible to overlook, but people in the room can nevertheless choose to behave as if the elephant is non-existent.

What is the symbolism of an elephant? Many African cultures revere the elephant and use it as a symbol of strength and power. In South Africa the elephant tusks are in their coat of arms to represent wisdom, strength, moderation, and eternity.

The elephant in the room refers to those issues or situations which nobody wants to address but they are there and at times can feel paralyzing. Sometimes it can be a sore spot; no one dares to touch it and so it is often ignored. Sometimes the elephants in the room arise out of those secrets, those experiences, thoughts and feelings that we keep from view. Some secrets by their very nature contain information that if disclosed could endanger lives or security. But then there are those secrets that if not shared or talked about openly can and often do become elephants in the room. These are those questions, problems, solutions, or issues that many of us know about but choose to ignore because to do so otherwise could cause embarrassment, sadness, or even trigger an argument. What happens to these types of secrets is that they many times they become elephants in the room.

Each day as I walked about in my neighborhood and in the city of Cape Town, I had the feeling as if I was that elephant in the room. I was that white

---

[2]Ivan Andreevich Krylov (1769-1844), poet and fabulist, wrote a fable entitled 'The Inquisitive Man' which tells of a man who goes to a museum and notices all sorts of tiny things, but fails to notice an elephant.

American who no matter how much tried to blend in was always noticeable. As the weeks rolled by, I experienced in a small sort of fashion what it feels like to be the minority person in the room. My color always stood out like marshmallows in a box of chocolates.

As I entered a room, restaurant or store being the only white American male, I wondered how many whispered conversations were directed toward me. This experience, along with living and working in a new country, without the comfort of familiar family and friends, weighed heavily upon my mind.

I felt like the elephant in the room that everyone noticed but that seemingly no one wanted to address or talk to. Each day I was keenly aware of my observations, but I allowed myself to be open and to look for opportunities to exchange a kind word or a greeting. Fortunately, I quickly learned some South African phrases and started on my early morning daily walks sharing them with those that I encountered. In English a common phase is: Good Morning! How are You? In Afrikaans that same phase is: *Goeie môre. Hoe gaan dit.* A common greeting by South Africans is *Ek sien jou en ek hoor jou.* Translated into English it means, I see you and I hear you.[3]

Yes, I was alone in a new place, a new country, and a new culture. However, as I let go of my own biases, I began to connect with those around me in meaningful ways. As I allowed my inner warmth to shine through, I quickly realized what was most important to the people of Cape Town — connections that were real and authentic.

I came to understand what being authentic means. For me it means that you act in ways that show your true self and how you feel. Rather than showing people only a particular side of yourself, you express your whole self genuinely. I have learned, and living in South Africa furthered my understanding, about how important being authentic is. Your authentic self is who you truly are as a person, regardless of your occupation, regardless of the influence of others; it is an honest representation of you. To be authentic means not caring what others think about you. This requires you to have a clear understanding of who you are and what you believe in.

---

[3]Afrikaans borrowed from other languages such as Portuguese, German, Malay, Bantu and Khoisan languages; see Sebba 1997, p. 160, Niesler, Louw & Roux 2005, p. 459.

My authentic self was tested many times during my time in South Africa. I learned to see people not by the color of their skin or their sexual identity but by who they are. I realized that our own identities are important because they allow us to connect with those who are like us. But our identities are not who we are. My mother always used to tell me: "we label jars, NOT people." I had a whole new appreciation for that profound statement. My work in the Cape Town community would allow me to meet and work with many people from a variety of cultural and ethnic backgrounds. This was never truer when Cape Town experienced a water crisis of large proportions.

Cape Town is one of the most multicultural cities in the world and is a significant destination for expatriates and immigrants. The ethnic and racial composition of Cape Town is: [4]

42.4% "Coloured"

38.6% "Black African"

15.7% "White"

1.4% "Asian or Indian"

1.9% other

The Cape Town Unitarian congregation was a good mix of cultures and people of color. In those first three months in South Africa, I arrived as summer was just beginning and the winter rains had been few and far between. The local area reservoirs that supplied the city of Cape Town and the surrounding areas with drinking water were only at 33 percent capacity going into the warm summer months. The local city officials were predicting that by early March the city would run out of water unless drastic action was taken.

The imminent action was water restrictions. Every person in each household was limited to just 50 liters of water per day, or just over 13 gallons. Water rationing was implemented, and the citizens of Cape Town reacted in a confused, critical manner. Bottled water at the grocery store was quickly scooped up and the citizens of Cape Town looked for other sources to obtain their water.

As the weeks moved along the date for Cape Town to run of water came and passed and kept moving. The citizens responded and water usage for the first time in years went down. The interfaith, an alliance of 35 faith communities,

---

[4]Statistics South Africa — City of Cape Town data and statistics

looked at ways in which they could bind together and teach the members of their congregations all about water conservation. This impossible task was taken on through a partnership with a local nonprofit called SAFCEI (Southern African Faith Communities Environment Institute). SAFCEI is a multi-faith organization committed to supporting faith leaders and their communities in Southern Africa by increasing awareness on critical action items like eco-justice, sustainable living, and climate change.

SAFCEI had developed a simple water audit for homes and businesses where the business leader or homeowner could use the audit to see where water was being wasted. The Interfaith alliance leaders received training from SAFCEI leaders that shared the information with each of our congregations.

Citizens of Cape Town responded and began to limit their daily water usage and became committed to looking for ways in which they could save water in their homes and businesses. I am one who loves a morning shower and while living in South Africa I learned how to conserve water. I would turn the shower on and get my body wet, then turn the shower off and soap up my body along with my hair. Then I would turn the shower back on and quickly rinse off, while collecting any excess water in a bucket that I had taken into the shower with me. Once finished showering I would pour the contents of the bucket into the toilet.

One of the things that I noticed was the disparity and the injustices that occurred to South Africans who were not as well off and who lived in parts of town that did not have full access to water and housing. To understand these disparities, one needs to understand a bit about the history of South Africa.

For many, particularly outside of South Africa, the name *Soweto* evokes an image by Sam Nzima made during the 1976 Soweto Uprising. In that iconic photograph, 18-year-old Mbuyisa Mahkubo carries Hector Pieterson, a 13-year-old boy who was fatally wounded when police fired on students protesting the official lowering of academic standards in South Africa's black schools. The image of the dying boy spread around the world, and today the uprising is widely seen as a turning point in the struggle against the nationalist government. "Soweto" became the symbol of the profound social, cultural, economic, and physical divisions of apartheid.[5]

But such a "black and white" reading underscores the complex spatial history of townships in South Africa. Soweto itself is not a unitary place but an abbreviation for Southwestern Townships, a collection of over 25 townships bordering Johannesburg's mining belt to the south, which range from middle-class enclaves to informal settlements (sometimes known as shantytowns). In South Africa, the terms township and location usually refer to the often underdeveloped racially segregated urban areas that, from the late 19th century until the end of apartheid, were reserved for non-whites, namely Indians, Africans and Coloureds.

Until the early 1990s, when South Africa became an inclusive democracy, nonwhite workers were forced to live outside cities in residential areas known as townships. The systematic segregation dates to the colonial era. In the late 19th and early 20th centuries, the British colonial government resettled racial groups under the pretense of responding to disease epidemics in overcrowded neighborhoods. The area now known as Soweto was settled by blacks and other nonwhites who were relocated after an outbreak of bubonic plague in central Johannesburg.

Early separation was formalized and reinforced by colonial laws such as the *Natives' Land Act of 1913*, which reserved nearly 90 percent of the land in South Africa for a tiny minority white population.[6] In the following decades, during which South Africa became an independent republic, a series of pass and influx laws comprehensively restricted the rights of the nonwhite population. During the Apartheid Era, from 1948 to 1994, the ruling Nationalist Party, dominated by white Afrikaaners, passed miscegenation laws, institutionalized legal segregation, formalized racial categories and restrictions on movement, and embedded apartheid physically in the landscape. Cities were designated "for whites only," and townships became, in effect, the mechanism for housing the nonwhite labor force. Such policies accelerated the growth of separate townships across the country at all scales — from cities like Cape Town and Johannesburg to the smallest villages.[7]

---

[5]Philip Bonner & Lauren Segal (1998). *Soweto: A History*. South Africa: Maskew Miller Longman
[6]Collins, Robert O. and James M. Burns: *A History of Sub-Saharan Africa*, p. 346. Cambridge University Press, 2007
[7]Krabill, Ron (2010). *Starring Mandela and Cosby: Media and the End(s) of Apartheid*. University of Chicago Press.

Khayalitsha, one of the townships outside of Cape Town is where over one million people live. To conserve water, the city of Cape Town turned off the water at all of the Khayalitsha car washes. The water they were using was recycled water and this action taken by the City of Cape Town served no purpose to conserve water and became a political crisis between Cape Town and the Township of Khayelitsha. A demonstration was called by one of the Interfaith leaders to sit in at the city council chambers. After three days the city turned back on the water at the car washes and the jobs of over 500 workers were restored.[8]

I was amazed at the power of protest and how in South Africa it still served as a powerful tool to bring awareness to issues that were affecting a group of marginalized people. I can still see the group of us sitting in the city council offices and standing up for the rights of others regarding water disparity.

A few weeks after this protest my ability to work through another conflict was called upon. It was the last Saturday in February, and it was a day to celebrate LGBTQ Pride. Many individuals had been planning, organizing, and working on making sure the Cape Town, South Africa pride parade and celebration went well. A group of 12 ordained ministers, including myself, from the various religious faiths in Cape Town, had been meeting and had decided that we would stand arm and arm at the beginning of the parade to show solidarity between the various religious faiths. The parade was scheduled to start at 10 a.m. and go along a pre-determined route and end up at the National Stadium.

It was a perfect summer day in Cape Town. The sun shone brightly in the sky that morning as the various groups who would march in the parade assembled. Our group gathered at the beginning of the parade and assisted on getting the various groups and individuals to line up in their previously assigned places. There was an excitement in the air as all of us eagerly waited for the festivities to begin.

About 45 minutes before was the moment that I shall never forget. The news leading up to this moment had included reports of numerous rapes, murders and other forms of abuse that had been carried out against young lesbian and

---

[8] *What It's Like To Live Through Cape Town's Massive Water Crisis*, By Aryn Baker

transgender women who were living and working in Khayalitsha, a Township located about 45 kilometers from Cape Town.

A LGBTQ+ organizer and advocate for the rights of lesbian and transgender women had arrived at the start of our parade with her supporters. They informed us that they were going to demonstrate and prevent the parade from happening. They felt that the needs of these women who had been raped, killed, and abused for coming out for being true to who they were being ignored. This group clearly stated that they would not move and that they wanted to stop the parade to bring attention to the deaths.

I turned to my colleagues, and we all wondered just what we could do. Finally, what seemed like an eternity but most likely was a few minutes an answer came. The leader of the group was approached and asked if we could have a full 10 minutes of silence before we started the parade as a recognition to honor the women who had been killed and maimed. Sparingly, the group agreed to our terms.

What happened next was pure magic. Our interfaith minister group walked the area where the groups were lined up for the parade. We asked them to please honor 10 minutes of silence. Within no time at all there was silence with all the groups that were gathered. At the six-minute mark I heard music coming from the next block. I ran over to investigate and saw a school bus. I quickly learned that this was a bus carrying LGBTQ+ people from Khayalitsha to the Gay Pride parade. I was able to stop the bus and quickly ask them to turn off their music. I explained to them that we were having a moment of silence for those who had been killed or maimed in Khayalitsha. A young woman at the back of the bus spoke up and said, "Thank you, I am one of those young people." I quickly learned that many of the young women on the bus had experienced the same abuse.

The group quietly left their bus and joined the group for the remaining 10 minutes of silence. The 10 minutes finished and quickly activity returned to the start of the parade groups. There was an excitement in the air but at the same time a new appreciation for those in the LGBTQ+ community who had given their life for standing up for who they were regarding their sexual identity. This experience has left a memory on my soul — showing that a group of people, regardless of race, religion or sexual orientation can come together and embrace and honor our LGBTQ+ brothers and sisters who stand up for who they are.

CHAPTER FOUR:

THE PEOPLE: A LESSON
IN FREEDOM

To understand the people of South Africa it is necessary to provide you with a lesson in history. Modern humans have lived at the southern tip of Africa for more than 100,000 years and their ancestors for some 3.3 million years. South Africa's history begins with the first humans that are believed to have inhabited South Africa more than 100,000 years ago.[9]

The first European settlement in southern Africa was established by the Dutch East India Company in Table Bay (Cape Town) in 1652. Created to supply passing ships with fresh produce, the colony grew rapidly as Dutch

---

[9]Lander, Faye; Russell, Thembi (2018). "The archaeological evidence for the appearance of pastoralism and farming in southern Africa

farmers settled to grow crops. Shortly after the establishment of the colony, slaves were imported from East Africa, Madagascar, and the East Indies.[10]

The Dutch developed the land, established new industries, created new jobs, drained the swamps, opened mines constructed canals and established trading partners. The Dutch also established a fort in Cape Town to be a settlement outpost for the trading ships that would pass around the Cape of Good Hope.[11]

The first British Settlers, known as the 1820 Settlers, arrived in Algoa Bay (now Nelson Mandela Bay) on board 21 ships, the first being the Chapman. They numbered about 4,500 and included artisans, tradesmen, religious leaders, merchants, teachers, bookbinders, blacksmiths, discharged sailors and soldiers, professional men and farmers.

In 1806, Britain occupied the Cape. As the colony prospered, the political rights of the various races were guaranteed. In 1867 diamonds were discovered near Kimberley in what is today known as the Northern Cape. The Kimberley diamond fields, and later discoveries along the Atlantic coast, emerged as major sources of gem-quality diamonds, securing South Africa's position as the world's leading producer in the mid-twentieth century.

In 1910, the Union of South Africa was created out of the Cape, Natal, Transvaal, and Free State. It was to be essentially a white union. Black opposition was inevitable, and the African National Congress (ANC) was founded in 1912 to protest the exclusion of black people from power.[12] In 1921, the South African Communist Party was established at a time of heightened militancy. More discriminatory legislation was enacted. Meanwhile, Afrikaner nationalism, fueled by job losses arising from a worldwide recession, was on the rise.

In 1948, the pro-Afrikaner National Party (NP) came to power with the ideology of apartheid, an even more rigorous and authoritarian approach than the previous segregationist policies. While white South Africa was cementing its power, black opposition politics were evolving. In 1943, a younger, more

---

[10] *History of Cape Colony before 1806 and History of South Africa* (1652–1815) Traders of the United East India Company (VOC), under the command of Jan van Riebieeck, were the first people to establish a European colony in South Africa. The Cape settlement was built by them in 1652 as a re-supply point and way-station for United East India Company vessels on their way back and forth between the Netherlands and Batavia (Jakarta) in the Dutch East Indies
[11] "*East India Company | Definition, History, & Facts | Britannica*".
[12] *History of the African National Congress.* In 1955, the Congress of the People officially adopted the Freedom Charter, stating the core principles of the South African Congress Alliance, which consisted of the African National Congress and its allies

determined political grouping came to the fore with the launch of the ANC Youth League, a development, which was to foster the leadership of people such as Nelson Rolihlahla Mandela, Oliver Tambo, and Walter Sisulu.

In 1944, Mandela, a lawyer, joined the African National Congress (ANC), where he became a leader of Johannesburg's youth wing of the ANC. In 1952, he became deputy national president of the ANC, advocating nonviolent resistance to apartheid. In 1960, Nelson helped organize a paramilitary branch of the ANC to engage in guerrilla warfare against the white minority government.

In 1961, he was arrested for treason, and although acquitted, he was arrested again in 1962 for illegally leaving the country. Convicted and sentenced to five years at Robben Island Prison, he was put on trial again in 1964 on charges of sabotage. In June 1964, he was convicted along with several other ANC leaders and sentenced to life in prison.[13]

Mandela spent the first 18 of his 27 years in jail at the Robben Island Prison. Confined to a small cell without a bed or plumbing, he was forced to do hard labor in a quarry. He could write and receive a letter once every six months, and once a year he was allowed to meet with a visitor for 30 minutes. However, Mandela's resolve remained unbroken, and while remaining the symbolic leader of the anti-apartheid movement, he led a movement of civil disobedience at the prison that coerced South African officials into drastically improving conditions on Robben Island. He was later moved to another location, where he lived under house arrest.

I had the opportunity to visit the prison where Nelson Mandela had been held for 18 years. Robbie Island, as it was called, sits out in the bay of Cape Town. It is only accessible by boat and is about a 45-minute boat ride from the city of Cape Town.

As I landed on the island a bus was waiting for our party to begin our tour. Our tour guide was a former prisoner. As we traveled around the island, he would point out the various buildings and share with us the history. The Island had its own power plant, a farm where all the food for the prisoners was grown, and a small manufacturing facility.

---

[13]"*Nelson Mandela 'breathing on his own'*". *News 24. 18 January 2011. Archived from the original on 25 February 2013. Retrieved 30 January 2011.*

As I listened to the guide talk, I could not help but visualize what life must have been like for Nelson Mandela. He had spoken up against the apartheid policies and was put into prison for life. The guide drove us by a pile of rocks that were stacked on top of each other. He explained that these had been put there by the former inmates as a symbol of their hope that one day they would be free.

The guide stopped the bus at the main part of the prison compound. He explained to us that we would be walking through the area where Nelson Mandela and other African National Congress members had been imprisoned.

I walked down very narrow, dark hallways and exceedingly small rooms. Then we came to the cell that had been Nelsons. I stopped and looked in and all that was in the room was a small table, small light, and no bed. Nelson Mandela had lived 18 of his 27 years in this cell.

I thought of the man, his mission, determination, and his vision. He believed in a free democratic society for South Africa. Much of the South African constitution Nelson composed while he was in prison. He made it his daily habit to study the US constitution and to read about our founding fathers. He based the concepts and principles in the South Africa constitution after Americas founding fathers.

Our tour of the prison concluded with the 'walk of freedom' — the symbolic journey that Nelson Mandela and his fellow inmates made upon their release from the main entrance of the prison to the harbor.[14]

As my partner Jerry and I took that walk I could not help but envision Nelson Mandela taking the same exact walk. A chill came over me as I strolled that walk of freedom. I thought about all the people that have taken that same walk. I felt a connection and a deeper appreciation and understanding of Nelson Mandela that day. I also reflected upon the many people in the U.S. who have and are spending time in our prisons for crimes that they did not commit.

I made a commitment that day that going forward in my life I would be a person that strived for justice in all my interactions. Touring Robbie Island and making that walk connected me to Nelson Mandela and I understood in a significant way the role that he played.

---

[14]Nelson Mandela: *Long Walk to Freedom*, p. 614. *Staff* (13 March 2009). *"Mandela's autobiography Long Walk to Freedom to be adapted into film*

Part of understanding the role that Nelson Mandela played in South African history is to understand what life under apartheid was like. From 1948 through the 1990s, a single word dominated life in South Africa. A apartheid — Afrikaans for *apartness* — this policy kept the country's majority Black population under the thumb of a small white minority. The rule affected every facet of life in South Africa and continued centuries-old patterns of discrimination, segregation, and racism.[15]

The segregation began in 1948 after the National Party came to power. The nationalist political party instituted policies of white supremacy, which empowered white South Africans who descended from both Dutch and British ancestry. The policy was designed to disenfranchise Black South Africans.

The system was rooted in the country's history of colonization and slavery. White settlers had historically viewed Black South Africans as a natural resource to be used to turn the country from a rural society to an industrialized one. Starting in the 17th century, Dutch settlers relied on slaves to build up South Africa. Around the time that slavery was abolished in the country in 1863, gold and diamonds were discovered in South Africa.

That discovery represented an opportunity for white-owned mining companies that employed Black workers to exploit them. Those companies all but enslaved Black miners while enjoying massive wealth from the diamonds and gold they mined. Like Dutch slave holders, they relied on intimidation and discrimination to rule over their Black workers.

The mining companies borrowed a tactic that earlier slaveholders and British settlers had used to control Black workers, pass laws. In South Africa, pass laws were a form of an integral passport system designed to segregate the population, manage urbanization, and allocate migrant labor. Also known as the natives' law, pass laws severely limited the movements of not only black African citizens, but other people as well — by requiring or designating areas only that white South Africans could shop, live, and congregate.

As early as the 18th century, these laws had required members of the Black majority, and other people of color, to carry identification papers at all times and restricted their movement in certain areas. They were also used to control

---

[15] *The Population Registration Act*, 1950, the basis for most apartheid legislation, was formally abolished in 1991,[1][2] although the country's first non-racial government was not established until multiracial elections held under a universal franchise in 1994.[3]

Black settlement, forcing Black people to reside in places where their labor would benefit white settlers.

Apartheid imposed heavy burdens on most South Africans. The economic gap between the wealthy few, nearly all of whom were white, and the poor masses, virtually all of whom were Black, Coloured, or Indian, was larger than in any other country in the world. While Whites generally lived well, Indians, Coloureds, and especially Blacks suffered from widespread poverty, malnutrition, and disease.

Most South Africans struggled daily for survival despite the growth of the national economy. On 30 March 1960, Philip Kgosanna led a Pan Africanist Congress (PAC) march of between 30,000-50,000 protestors from Langa and Nyanga to the police headquarters in Caledon Square, in the heart of the city of Cape Town. The protesters offered themselves up for arrest for not carrying their passes. Police were temporarily paralyzed with indecision. Kgosana agreed to disperse the protestors if a meeting with J B Vorster, then Minister of Justice, could be secured. He was tricked into dispersing the crowd and was arrested by the police later that day.[16]

On the same day, the government responded by declaring a state of emergency and banning all public meetings. The police and army arrested thousands of Africans, who were imprisoned with their leaders, but still the mass action raged. The Minister of Native Affairs declared that apartheid was a model for the world. The Minister of Justice called for calm and the Minister of Finance encouraged immigration. The only Minister who showed any misgivings regarding government policy was Paul Sauer.

A week after the state of emergency was declared, the African National Congress (ANC) and the PAC were banned under the Unlawful Organizations Act of 8 April 1960. Both organizations were deemed a serious threat to the safety of the public. The imposition of a state of emergency, the arrest of thousands of Black people and the banning of the ANC and PAC convinced the anti-apartheid leadership that non-violent action was not going to bring about change without armed action. The ANC and PAC were forced underground and operated that way until 1994.[17]

---

[16]Ayodele Langley, *Pan-Africanism and Nationalism in West Africa 1900-1945* (Oxford, 1973)

[17]*The Unlawful Organizations Act* (No. 34 of 1960) was security legislation by which the government of apartheid South Africa banned the African National Congress and the Pan Africanist Congress. It subjected them to the same banning regime already applied to the South African Communist Party under the Suppression of Community

In 1986, the international community strengthened its support for the anti-apartheid cause. Mass resistance increasingly challenged the apartheid State, which resorted to intensified repression accompanied by eventual recognition that apartheid could not be sustained.

South Africa held its first democratic election in April 1994 under an interim Constitution. The ANC emerged with a 62% majority. South Africa was divided into nine new provinces to replace the four existing provinces and 10 black homelands. The second democratic election, in 1999, saw the ANC increasing its majority to a point just short of two-thirds of the total vote.[18]

In the April 2004 election, the ANC won the national vote with 68% and the celebration of Ten Years of Freedom was attended by heads of state and government delegations from across the world.

The rich history of South Africa helped me to better understand the people, the culture, and the challenges that they have had to face and are currently facing. The practice of apartheid influenced the people — especially the non-whites. During Apartheid, all decisions were made for the mass of classes. The non-whites could only live in designated sections of the city. If people were white, they were protected but if they were classified as non-white, they faced tremendous discrimination.

Even though apartheid and its policies ended over 15 years ago the effect of that policy still can be seen clearly in the lives of the South African people. For many too young or too distant to remember, apartheid is little more than a vague historical fact, a system of forced segregation to learn about in history class, to condemn and to move on.

But for South Africans who survived the decades of punishing racial classification, humiliating work rules, forced relocation and arbitrary treatment by authorities, the end of apartheid was the birth of an entirely new world, midwifed in large part by Nelson Mandela. And that is his lasting legacy.

In 2018 South Africa declared it as the Year of Mandela in that year Nelson would have turned 100 years old. But although Nelson Mandela died in 2013 at the age of 95, his entire life still stands as a testament to the power of the human spirit.

---

[18]Mafika (8 May 2014). "A look back at national election results – Brand South Africa"

Here are seven ways Nelson Mandela's legacy continues:[19]

- Citizens hold dearly, including women's empowerment, access to quality education, and the fight against HIV/AIDS.
- He ushered hundreds of women into the political sphere. Though South Africa has work to do to eliminate violence against women and to ensure that women earn the same amount of money as men, Mandela helped set the country on a path toward equality from the very beginning of his career as president.
- He joined the fight against HIV/AIDS. In 2000, as the scope of the crisis became overwhelmingly evident, Mandela added his voice to the chorus of activists calling for recognition of the disease and action to prevent it.
- He brought education to rural students. In 2007, Mandela founded the Nelson Mandela Institute for Rural Development and Education to train and send high-quality teachers to rural areas.
- He fought for children. During his tenure as President, Mandela donated a third of his salary to create the Nelson Mandela Children's Fund.
- He promoted scientific and environmental education. Mandela so valued the power of science and research that he lent his name to three institutes of technology in Nigeria, Tanzania, and Burkina Faso.
- He expanded voting rights to all South Africans. "The Africans require, want the franchise, the basis of One Man One Vote — they want political independence," he said.
- He fought for peace and justice around the world.

South Africa today remains a country that has celebrated over 20 years of democracy and freedom. Many issues from the Coronavirus, to jobs, to economic inequality, face the nation today. South African people are resilient and will continue to learn from their past and celebrate their future. A new generation is rising up and taking advantage of the opportunities that are ever-present.

Over two decades after the end of apartheid, there is still a vast gulf between the experiences of South Africa's white students and black students. Today, South Africa remains one of the most unequal countries in the world, a place

---

[19]Nelson Mandela by Phineas Rueckert, and David Brand at Global Citizen

where poverty breaks down largely along racial lines. A black person is four times more likely to be unemployed than a white person, and the average income for a white family is six times greater than for a black family.

South Africa is also experiencing the continent's so-called "youth bulge," with 66% of its own population under the age of 35. While this generation may not have witnessed the injustice of Apartheid firsthand, they are enduring the burden of its aftermath — a struggle for opportunities.

Despite its status as an emerging global power, South Africa is one of the most unequal countries in the world, impeding the ability of young people from less advantaged backgrounds to access opportunities in terms of skills development, higher education, and professional training.

However, what I found, as I met with young South Africans, is strong sense of agency among South Africa's youth. I discovered that the young South Africans (ages 18-25) generally believe that their future will be brighter, and that getting more involved in networks and social movements is crucial to building resilience and opening new job prospects. They want to "stay woke" to changing external circumstances and take control over their own lives through social action as well as political participation.[20] Attitudes towards education are also changing, with 83% of young people believing that TVET (technical and vocational education and training) will help them to find a job.

Some of the many problems South Africa now faces — such as the conflict over land ownership — predate apartheid, but by far the majority can be traced to that era. Most obviously, the impoverished townships and weak educational system are the result of decades of spending policies that deliberately left black South African communities underdeveloped. However, the current style of governance and the normalization of corruption began during the apartheid era as well. Those legacies have been difficult to escape and continue to bedevil the country today.

I have great hope in the next generations of South Africans. They have been taught the history of their predecessors and they desire to make a difference. I found the rising generation to be very much awake to the opportunities that they have for education and hope to make a difference. The next generation is

---

[20]Staying Awoke, The struggle for opportunity in South Africa; British Council; April 2018

showing up and is engaged with making changes happen in government policies and in holding their leaders accountable. Nelson's Mandela's legacy is very much alive today in South Africa.

CHAPTER FIVE:

WHAT I LEARNED FROM
THE TOWNSHIPS

The opportunity to visit, to teach and to meet with South Africans and others in townships was a great cultural learning experience for me. I remember the first time I visited the township called Khayelitsha, along N2 road near Cape Town. The very first thing I noticed were the beautiful blooming blue jacaranda trees. Shortly after spotting the trees, however, I noticed a mixture of houses and shanty dwellings built of scrap metal, cardboard, and anything else available. This image created quite a contrast and served as my visual introduction to the South African Township called Khayelitsha.[21]

---

[21]Khayelitsha (/ˌkaɪ.ə'liːtʃə/) is a township in Western Cape, South Africa, on the Cape Flats in the City of Cape Town. The name is Xhosa for *New Home*. It is reputed to be the larges and fastest-growing township in South Africa.

My first entry into the Khayelitsha Township was to meet a group of women at their neighborhood community center. These women were known for their beaded crafts. I was excited to meet them, see their creations and learn about their entrepreneurial businesses. On the way to the neighborhood center, we passed by several schools, makeshift housing dwellings and numerous small businesses, and all appeared to be thriving.

I was amazed by the spirit of entrepreneurship that I saw. Small businesses seemed to have sprung up in unused containers, mostly metal sheds that had been thrown together. Sometimes there were no other spaces available, just empty pieces of land. I passed by auto repair shops, hair and beauty salons, craft markets, restaurants, and taverns. I witnessed a bustling, vibrant positivity and people who were friendly and seemed to be very happy.

When I arrived at the Neighborhood Community Center I was greeted by their Executive Director, who was a native South African and who by South African assessment was considered mixed (meaning both Black and White are part of their heritage). When we stepped inside the building it was explained to us that a portion of their new addition was financed by a Jewish Congregation out of New York City.

This was a Women's Neighborhood Center. My partner and I were ushered into a room where the women gathered worked with beads, various types of art, purses, and other craft items. They were happy to show us their creations and to share with us how they made them. Most of these women were in their sixties and seventies and their smiles and spirit were contagious.

I learned from the women that when many of them had become more successful, they still chose to stay in the township to be close to their family roots rather than move to a more affluent suburb. In a broken English accent, many of the women explained to me that they believed that the township was a lot safer than how it was portrayed in the media. Many of the women shared with me that they just wanted to live in peace and to do the best they can. I found them all to be overwhelmingly friendly and cheerful.

It appeared to me that despite the various pitfalls of township life, the people, overall, were more than capable of rising to the challenges. I heard amazing stories of selflessness and generosity: orphanages run on a shoestring and a prayer by people who do not have enough resources of their own; schools run voluntarily by retired teachers with little to no materials at their disposal; soup kitchens organized by tireless charity workers for people who might well have only that one meal every day. I found rare human beings who dedicated their entire lives to helping their fellow man, despite their disadvantages.

In South Africa, the terms township and location usually referred to the often-underdeveloped, segregated urban areas. From the late 19th century until the end of apartheid, these sections were reserved for non-whites, namely Indians, Africans and Coloureds. Townships were usually built on the outskirts of towns and cities. The term township also has a distinct legal meaning in South Africa's system of land title, which carries no racial connotations. In other words, no title or claim to the land.[22]

During the first half of the twentieth century in South Africa, a clear major-ity of the black population in major urban areas lived in hostels or servant's accommodations provided by employers and were mostly single men. In the period during and following World War II, urban areas of South Africa experi-enced a rapid period of urbanization as the color bar was relaxed due to the war. Neither employers nor the government built new accommodation or homes for the influx of new residents. This led to overcrowding, poor living conditions, and the absence of amenities such as housing, water, electricity, and sewage. High rents and overcrowding led to land invasions and the growth of shack settlements, which were largely ignored by the government.

During the era of apartheid, black people were evicted from properties that were in areas designated as "white only" and forced to move into segregated townships. Separate townships were established for each of the three designated non-white race groups — Black people, Coloureds and Indians.

Today, most South African towns and cities have at least one township associated with them. Township communities are faced with several social problems. Most often, the residents of townships do not own the land on which their houses are built. Construction is informal and unregulated by the

---

[22]In South Africa, the terms **township** and **location** usually refer to the often underdeveloped racially segregated urban areas that, from the late 19th century until the end of apartheid, were reserved for non-whites, namely Indians, Africans and Coloureds. Townships were usually built on the periphery of towns and cities. Pettman, Charles (1913). *Africanderisms; a glossary of South African colloquial words and phrases and of place and other names.* Longmans, Green and Co. p. 298.

government. This results in a lack of access to basic services such as sewage, electricity, roads, and clean water.

The sewer systems within the townships are poorly planned and constructed. The population of the townships typically grows faster than the infrastructure was planned for, causing overloads that result in blockages, surges, and overflows. A consequence of inadequate pumping infrastructure and large populations is that water pressure in townships is low. There are often a limited number of public toilets that are over-used, abused, and quickly become health hazards for the community.

There is normally one pump within each section of the townships. Water is used for everything from washing clothes, cooking, drinking, bathing, and housecleaning. Having very little water available for each section makes it very challenging to obtain enough water for a day per household.

Electrical wires strung along the trees leading to power boxes are an abundant sight in the townships due to illegal electricity connections. Most of the substations are very unsecured to begin with so having so many additional wires coming off of them is very dangerous for the people nearby and the kids playing in the area.

Backyard shacks are additional units on a plot of land that are rented out by the landowner for additional income. A plot of land designed for a house big enough for one family has turned into a plot of land that holds on average of six families instead of one. These structures are illegally built in violation of planning and building codes and strain infrastructure. Governments are loathed to act on backyard dwellings; doing so would result in a large-scale displacement of people.

Township schools are often overcrowded and lack adequate infrastructure. There is a high dropout rate of poor youth, particularly around Grade 9. Despite government interventions, education outcomes remain skewed, with township students continuing to perform poorly. This skewed distribution is mainly attributable to higher and more rapid dropout rates among the poor, rather than to a lack of initial access to schooling. The formerly white schools uniformly produce better results. Their governing bodies can raise substantial private funds to get resources that are then unreachable by the rural and township schools which survive on the commitment of their teachers.[23]

Gangs are a problem in townships, and children as young as 12 or 13 will begin initiation into a local gang. Some see violence and gangs as a way of life and culture. The weapon of choice for most is a gun and with easy accessibility, anyone is able to obtain one. It is estimated that out of the 14 million guns in circulation, in South Africa, only four million are registered and licensed to legal gun owners.

I learned that although South Africa is ranked as an upper middle-income economy by the World Bank, nearly half of the country's urban population live in townships. Today, these informal settlements are home to nearly 60% of South Africa's unemployed.

The South African economy is the second largest in Africa and accounts for almost a quarter of the continent's GDP. The economy has almost tripled since the end of international sanctions with the demise of apartheid in 1996. However, today, South Africa continues to battle high unemployment, great levels of income inequality, corruption, and more recently, political mismanagement, amongst other challenges.[24]

I had the opportunity to visit another township called Langa, which is located on the outskirts of Cape Town under the shadow of Table Mountain. It was there that I met my guide Naati. Langa is one of many townships in Cape Town that were designated for Black Africans before the apartheid era. For well over two hours, Naati, my guide for the afternoon, showed me a unique cultural experience that I will never forget.

The ramshackle houses, graffiti-covered walls, and shabbily constructed corner shops that I witnessed as we strolled through Langa were in stark contrast to the ocean-view villas perched on the seaside cliffs in Cape Town. Though I expected to find this dissimilarity, I did not expect to experience the rich atmosphere and energy that reverberated across this Township community.

The fact that it was 3pm on a weekday did not prevent Langa to be abuzz with loud music, house parties, and family gatherings with more than a fair share of alcohol. "The friendships and bonds that I have here, I can never

---

[23]Clark, Nancy L.; William H. Worger (2016). *South Africa : the rise and fall of apartheid* (Third ed.). Abingdon, Oxon. ISBN 978-1-138-12444-8. OCLC 8836492

[24]Silver, Caleb. "The Top 20 Economies in the World". *Investopedia*. Retrieved 2020-05-09.

replace with anything," Naati beamed with a smile. That is all well and good. However, with bustling Cape Town a stone's throw away, I could not understand why the local residents chose to stay in Langa earning little money as opposed to exploring more stable opportunities in the city. "People work not to leave Langa but to stay in the township and make it better," Naati explained. He proudly pointed to what he described to be Cape Town's Beverley Hills: a level-paved lane within the township surrounded by beautifully designed houses, complete with luxury cars in the driveway. This was the more affluent part of the township, home to the burgeoning upper middle class of Langa that has cultivated during the past couple of decades. "That is what we all want, that is what we aspire to achieve — without ever leaving Langa!" he exclaimed.

Entrepreneurship is the primary avenue for income for Langa's residents. Internet cafes, home repairs, vehicle maintenance, electrical installations, and manufacturing are just some of the local business ventures that entrepreneurs are picking up on. Walking around Langa, I could not help but notice the potential that townships such as Langa could offer to South Africa's large corporations. With a little capital injection, this potential could certainly be harnessed.[25]

As we made our way deep into the inner streets, we were trailed by soft giggles of children playing on the streets under the bright sunshine, their faces beaming with curiosity. They waved at us from a distance perhaps not sure of what to expect in return. It was not long before the waves turned into high fives and fist pumps. Each approached us with slight apprehension that gradually dissolved with Naati's constant encouragement. Then, one of the kids described Marc, a master's student at the Cornell Institute for Public Affairs, as the 'Black American.' At that moment, none of us could contain our laughter and our smiles gave the children greater confidence to approach us. After a moment of a cultural exchange with our pint-sized acquaintances, the youngsters were off on another exploration for the day while we continued our neighborhood tour.

Our next destination was a hostel, a prime example of how dwellings were constructed with a focus on maximum occupancy rather than functionality and design. The hostel was a 6-bedroom unit with a capacity to accommodate

---

[25]Gordon Institute of Business Science, University of Pretoria, Understanding the Township Entrepreneur,

16 men. Over time, as the men married, the hostel became home to 16 families — with an average of 4 people per family, for a total of 64 people! Yes, 64 people living in a 6-bedroom unit. As we toured the rooms, Naati explained how the parents and the youngest child sleep on the bed, while other kids sleep on mattresses on the ground. "People may live in sheds but wear nice clothes and drive nice cars to show others that you are doing well," Naati explained. The discussion then turned to other facets of the people and their traditions.

"The best life is in a hostel. People who like to complain love living in a hostel because there is so much to complain. But this makes people more positive and adapt to make themselves happy. They learn to be tolerant towards other people, socialize with them, and appreciate small things while constantly telling themselves that there are bigger things out there to achieve," concluded Naati.

As we walked across Langa, I could not help but notice the freedom and independence the township's residents enjoyed, despite the poverty and unemployment that plagues their community. The people of Langa enjoy living a simple life. They embrace the township as their own and forge lasting relationships with each other. Nothing typified this more than Naati exchanging greetings and banter with everyone he came across — adults and children alike — at every corner. Such community bonds I believe thrust Langa forward and are a sign of its remarkable resilience and independent spirit.

The face of South African townships is changing, as more and more poor white people are moving into formerly black-only neighborhoods. Township's physical presence are also changing. Soweto, for example, one of the South Africa's biggest townships, is expanding and developing rapidly. Today, it is not only a residential area with simple brick houses and cheaply made huts, it offers skyscrapers, malls, restaurants, businesses, stadiums and parks. In the last ten years alone, the government has invested a lot of money into making South Africa's former townships more livable. In addition, the government is providing more and more services, schools, and clean water.

I am grateful that I had the opportunity to experience two of South Africa's Townships. I shall always remember the people, the excitement, and the spirit of entrepreneurship. It served as a good reminder of the spirit of creativity that always unfolds when we take the time to open our minds and our hearts to new ways of thinking and being in the world.

It also reminds me of the importance of community and engagement with the neighborhood where one works, lives, or is a part of. I witnessed first-hand the love, the connection, and the bonds of friendship that naturally occur in a community where people genuinely care about each other. In America, people so often equate money with happiness. But all the money in the world won't make a person happy if they don't have a sense of community and connection. In South Africa, where many people are living in extreme poverty, the sense of shared spirit is something money can't buy.

CHAPTER SIX:

THE POWER OF MUSIC IN STORY

From the earliest colonial days until the present time, South African music has created itself out of the blending of local philosophies and customs with those introduced from outside the country, giving it all a special twist that carries with it the unmistakable flavoring of the country.

In the Dutch colonial era, from the 17th century on, indigenous tribespeople and slaves imported from the East adapted Western musical instruments and ideas. The Khoi-Khoi, for instance, developed the ramkie, a guitar with three or four strings, based on that of Malabar slaves, and used it to blend Khoi and Western folk songs.[26]

---

[26]Elphick, Richard. 1977. *Khoikhoi and the Founding of White South Africa*. London.

The missionary influence, plus the later influence of American spirituals, spurred a gospel movement that is still very strong in South Africa today. Drawing on the traditions of churches such as the Zion Christian Church, the Zion Christian Church (or ZCC) is one of the largest African-initiated churches operating across Southern Africa. The church's headquarters are at Zion City Moria in Limpopo Province (old Northern Transvaal), South Africa.

Possibly the best-known South African music style is Isicathamiya, which is a singing style that originated from the South African Zulus. The word itself does not have a literal translation; it is derived from the Zulu verb *cathama*, which means walking softly, or tread carefully. Isicathamiya choirs are traditionally all males. Its roots reach back before the turn of the 20th century, when numerous men left the homelands to search for work in the cities.[27]

Isicathamiya was developed after World War I as a secular a cappella choral singing with coordinated dance moves. It grew out of a blending of Zulu music with Western choral styles and other South African influences.

The missionary emphasis on choirs, combined with the traditional vocal music of South Africa, and taking in other elements as well, also gave rise to a mode of acapella singing that blended the style of Western hymns with indigenous harmonies. This vocal music is the oldest traditional music known in South Africa.

The music scene in South Africa is focused around four major areas: Johannesburg, Cape Town, Durban, and Bloemfontein. One of the characteristics of the scene is the strong sense of community — which sees artists, promoters, and venues all actively involved in developing the local talent.

When I think about South African Music, I remember the concert that I attended where a Zulu international performer from Zimbabwe, Oliver Mtukudzi, one of Zimbabwe's most renowned musicians, performed. A group of us from the Unitarian church decided we wanted to experience a live performance. Our seats were located on the second row in the middle. When Oliver came out onto the stage, a roar from the crowd occurred and everyone around us stood up and started singing phrases in what I soon learned was the Zulu language.

---

[27]Levine, Laurie (2005). *The Drumcafe's Traditional Music of South Africa*. Jacana. pp. 62–72.

More than two-thirds of the audience that night was Zimbabwe's who were now living in South Africa. They treated Oliver as if he was the King of music. His songs were uniquely African. The concert was scheduled to last for two hours. Oliver kept playing and singing and the show finally ended well past the two-hour mark.

The music inspired lots of audience participation. He would play a few chords and then turn to the audience and ask us to sing back to him. The enthusiastic crowd responded by singing and dancing and doing all types of body movement. I sat behind two women who were from Zimbabwe, and they turned around and offered to teach me just how to dance to the music.

After a few short lessons they left me to figure out to how to dance to their music. I tried to put into place the new ways to move that the nice women had taught me. The moves were like that of the Hawaiian Hula. The kind woman turned around from her seat in front of me and watched me try to do the dance moves that she had taught me. She laughed and said to me, "you just need to loosen up and feel the music and the beat." It took me a while but finally I was able to move and groove the way that she had taught me. As I looked around, everyone in the venue was standing up and they were all moving and grooving to the beat of the music. I had been to a lot of concerts in the US, but never once did I witness what I experienced that evening with everyone dancing; the musical sounds seemed to go on forever.

I have thought back upon this experience with the South African music and culture several times; each time a calm happy feeling comes over me as I remember the crowd that night and the two young South African women who tried to teach a White man to move and groove.

Today, there are dozens of popular musical styles and genres in the country that include Blues Rock, Trance, Hip-Hop, Soul, Jazz, Pop, and many other forms. South African Music reflects a complex history of African and Western cultures, and of conflict and perseverance.

The country of South Africa sits at the very southern end of the African continent. It's home to many indigenous cultures. I am defining *Indigenous* as the people who are originally native to a particular geographic location.[28] In

---

[28] *"Indigenous definition"*. Merriam-Webster. 2021.

South African culture, the Khoisan (a group made of two peoples, the Khoi, and the San), are considered indigenous. Their musical sounds are made up of polyphonic chants in which multiple independent melodies are sung at the same time. Another Indigenous people are the KwaXhosa and the Zulu (also made up of several ethnic groups). They have strong oral musical traditions, with women performing songs and dances for ceremonies. Many of these cultures also use a variety of musical instruments like drums, rattles, and other percussions, as well as strings and some winds like flutes.[29]

Until quite recently, there were two completely different music scenes in South Africa. One was the music of the Whites, which had its roots in European music. The other was the music of the Black population, born of a long ethnic tradition. This music must be lived through participation: singing, dancing, clapping, or banging a drum.

These days, the two groups are influenced by each other and by music from all around the world. The blend that arises from these diverse cultural influences is evident in all music forms. A good example is Kwaito, which is a mixture of house music, R&B, Jamaican Reggae, and American Hip-Hop. Yet the language, lyrics and the style of dancing and dressing are distinct to South African townships.[30]

The very popular choral music and township jazz and blues have also adopted sounds from other cultures. These unique mixtures have attracted international attention. For example, the singer Miriam Makeba, the jazz pianist Abdullah Ibrahim, and the jazz trumpeter Hugh Masekela are internationally well-known.

Opera, musicals, and classical music are also strongly represented in the country. The diversity of South African music is celebrated in several festivals throughout the year. The variety of the events in South Africa reflects the assortment of the country so rich with diversity in everything from language to arts and culture. You can find anything from a burn in the desert to cultural exhibitions in the city and a music festival to ring in the New Year.

---

[29]Nombembe, Caciswa. "Music-making of the Xhosa diasporic community: a focus on the Umguyo tradition in Zimbabwe." Masters' dissertation, School of Arts, Faculty of Humanities, University of the Witwatersrand, 2013.

[30]Coffee, Black. "A Chat with Black Coffee — Kwaito is Still Around". *XLR8R*. xlr8r.com. Archived from the original on 12 January 2008. Retrieved 5 December 2007.

One of the first musical festivals celebrations that my partner Jerry and I attended was on New Year's Eve. We had been told that the various city neighborhoods in Cape Town all participated in this festival which lasts until the 2nd of January. The locals call it their New Year's Carnival. The New Year's Carnival is a multifaceted celebration of life, rite of renewal, and festival of music, involving minstrel troupes, Malay choirs, and Christmas bands.

In many ways, the New Year's Carnival is like Carnival in Rio de Janeiro, and Mardi Gras in New Orleans. Unlike those events, however, Cape Town's celebration is not tied to the Christian calendar. It owes its timing to Emancipation Day — the day on which the slaves were freed in South Africa, in the 1830s — and, of course, to the birth of the New Year.

One of the most visible aspects of the Carnival is the night march by Malay choirs [*nagtroepe* or night troupes] through central Cape Town. The other highlight is the minstrel troupes' parade along the same route, on the 2nd of January [*die Tweede Nuwe Jaar* or the Second New Year].[31]

Minstrel troupes are clubs [*klopse*] created by people who love Carnival and its traditions. Troupe members participate in various ways–in the bands and choirs, as part of the marching teams, as dancers, and as ordinary members, carrying umbrellas and jollying through the streets. Membership is open to men and women as well as boys and girls. Members of the various troupes wear colorful uniforms that are specific to each troupe.

Malay choirs are also clubs of a sort. They take their name from an eighteenth-century colonial term, "Malay,[32]" that was applied to one segment of the Cape Town population: slaves and political exiles brought to South Africa from what is now Malaysia and Indonesia by the Dutch East India Company. Male descendants of Malays make up a substantial proportion of the choirs' membership. The choirs perform a variety of songs that range from old Dutch folk songs to comic songs [*moppies*] to American pop songs. The sounds of the choirs reveal the influence of Asian and Islamic singing styles. The choirs are accompanied by instrumentalists playing guitars, mandolins, banjos, the traditional *ghoema* drum, and sometimes other stringed instruments. When the choirs march through central Cape Town on New Year's Eve, wearing track

---

[31] *Senses of Culture – South African Culture Studies*. Edited by Sarah Nuttall and Cheryl-Ann Michael. Oxford University Press 2000. pp. 363-379. "Cape Town's Coon Carnival". Dennis Constant Martin
[32]??

suits, they are referred to as *nagtroepeor* night troupes. When they appear on stage in competition, wearing sober suits and ties, they resume their identity as Malay choirs. Many members of the minstrel troupe choirs are also members of Malay choirs.[33]

Jerry and I experienced the various troupes marching through the city of Cape Town on New Year's Eve. We heard the musical sounds and witnessed the marching about. If you have ever been to Mardi Gras in New Orleans or to the Mummer's parade on New Year's Day in Philadelphia, take the different types of music and costumes and you have something similar in the Malay Choirs. Each group has a unique costume as well as a musical sound that is unique to their group.

It was truly a kaleidoscopic of sounds that we heard and delighted in on New Year's Eve. On the eve of January 1st, we saw people gather in the *Bo-Kaap* (Malay Quarter in Signal Hill) to await the *Tweede Nuwe Jaar* (2 January). The songs of Malay choirs and *ghoema* drums could be heard as the various troupes ushered in the dawn of a New Year. We learned that this celebration could trace its beginning back to the 19th century.[34]

During the 19th century, the New Year celebrated by the Dutch was the biggest annual feast. Slaves would get a day off on January 2nd and were allowed to celebrate in their own manner. Slavery was officially abolished in the Cape on December 1st, 1834. The *Tweede Nuwe Jaar*[35] became a celebration that united the "creole culture" in Cape Town. It is estimated that the first carnival troupe was organized in 1887. In the Apartheid years the Cape Minstrels sang songs like "Dis'n nuwe jaar" (It's a New Year), and many local songs, which were truer to the Cape Province and the local milieu.

Modern Cape Minstrel tradition was influenced by the visit to the Cape by American Minstrels. Old Cape minstrels, such as "The Ethiopians," had their own collection of Dutch and American songs. These Minstrels used to parade the streets of Cape Town and serenade the locals with their songs.

---

[33]"Cape Malay | South African History Online". V1.sahistory.org.za. Archived from the original on 4 October 2011. Retrieved 12 May 2013.

[34]*Senses of Culture – South African Culture Studies*. Edited by Sarah Nuttall and Cheryl-Ann Michael. Oxford University Press 2000. pp. 363-379. "Cape Town's Coon Carnival". Dennis Constant Martin

[35]?

In 1862, the then-internationally renowned Christy's Minstrels visited the Cape from the United States. The Christy's Minstrels were White men and women who had blackened their faces with burnt cork to impersonate the African American slaves. Between July 1890 and June 1898, they staged many Minstrels shows in Cape Town and it is believed that this contributed to the birth of the Cape Minstrels and the Carnival.[36]

In 1921, the Cape Town Cricket Club held a rival carnival in Newlands. This was the start of minstrel competitions in various venues and by various organizing boards. New Year's Carnivals of the 1920s and 1930s brought Minstrels, Privates, Brass Bands, Choirs and Malay Choirs together.

While my partner Jerry and I watched the events of a new year evolve, I could not help but think what a privilege it was for us to be experiencing a part of the local Cape Town culture. I wanted to learn more about the celebration. A few days later after researching on Google I discovered the following history.

Cape Malays, also known as Cape Muslim or Malays, are a Muslim community or ethnic group in South Africa. They are the descendants of enslaved and free Muslims from different parts of the world who lived at the Cape during Dutch and British rule.

Although the initial members of the community were from the Dutch colonies of Southeast Asia, by the 1800s, the term Malay encompassed all practicing Muslims at the Cape, regardless of origin. They initially used Malay as a language of religious instruction and are referred to as *Malays*.[37]

Malays are concentrated in the Cape Town area. Cape Malay cuisine forms a significant part of South African cuisine, and the community played an important part in the history of Islam in South Africa. The Dutch East India Company founded and established a colony at the Cape of Good Hope, as a supply station for ships travelling between Europe and Asia, which developed into the city of Cape Town. The Cape Malay community's earliest members were enslaved Javanese people transported by the Dutch East India Company to the Cape.

---

[36] *Toll, Robert.C (1974). Blacking Up: The Minstrel Show in Nineteenth-century America. Oxford University Press. ISBN 978-0-19-502172-1. Foster and the Christy Ministrels*

[37] *"Ethnic Group (eng)". indonesia.go id. Indonesian Information Portal. 2017. Retrieved 29 December 2020. This quantity only provides the ethnic group population that lies under the term "Melayu" of Melayu Asahan, Melayu Deli, Melayu Riau, Langkat/ Melayu Langkat, Melayu Banyu Asin, Asahan, Melayu, Melayu Lahat, and Melayu Semendo in some part of Sumatra*

I enjoyed learning more about this aspect of Cape Town culture. It helped to prepare me for an event that the Cape Town Unitarian Church congregation helped to organize. A Unitarian Church Choir from San Francisco, California reached out to our congregation and asked if they could work with the Unitarian Church in Cape Town to do a joint choir performance. The San Francisco choir would be brining 65 members along with their director and accompanist. The Unitarian Church choir in Cape Town was a small group composed of 10 choir members.

It was decided that one of the joint numbers both choirs would perform together was a Zulu Number called "*Siyahamba*", and that it would be performed in the native language of Zulu. The title means "We Are Marching" or "We are Walking" in the Light of God.[38]

Although "*Siyahamba*" has been associated with the anti-apartheid movement, it was not composed as a protest song, however. After its introduction to Europe and the US in the 1980s, it was often used in the international effort to end the regime of racial discrimination in South Africa. Nowadays, "*Siyahamba*" is viewed both locally and internationally as a liberation song. As such, it is still performed not only in church and at concerts, but also at rally's, demonstrations, and processions, sometimes with the lyrics modified to match the theme of the event. In this way, the historic South African tune continues to contribute to current struggles for change.

"Siyahamba" is often performed by children's groups in both sacred and secular environments. Occasionally, the translated lyrics are modified for a secular performance: for example, the English translation "We are marching in the light of God" becomes "We are standing in the light of peace."

As the weeks approached for our Cape Town Unitarian Church choir and the Unitarian choir from San Francisco would be performing, I began to plan and work out all the details so that the occasion would be a community event and a great spiritual experience for all who tuned in and who were present that day.

My team and I had quite a task ahead of us. We had to find a way that we could fit a choir of 65 members along with 50 of our members and our choir of

---

[38]Gorelik, Boris (2020). "'Siyahamba': The Origins and Significance of a South African Chorus". *Muziki*. **17** (2): 3-

10 into our small church, which only could hold around 100 people. I enlisted the aid of a member who used a computer program to come up with a diagram as to how we could lay out the chairs and in the format that would provide us with the maximum amount of use of space.

We had to rent over 60 chairs and once they were delivered to the church our next task began. We had to set up the chairs according to the diagram that had been generated. We followed the diagram and were able to set up all chairs. As the member and I looked out over what we had set up a calm and peaceful feeling came over me. I felt a relaxed sense that all would be ok.

The day came and the service unfolded. I had asked a South African family to perform a musical choir number to start our worship service. While they were singing in their own native tongue a spirit of love poured out over the hall. I felt the presence of the past leadership of the Cape Town Unitarian church that had passed on. I felt the love of all those who had gathered that morning in our hall.

Our worship service progressed, and I was able to honor one of the past Unitarian Ministers who had served the congregation. The revered Carpenter had passed away the previous day and he had served the Unitarian congregation during the Apartheid years and had opened the church doors to all people regardless of the color of their skin. We shared a moment of silence for him and for his family.

The time had come in the service for our small Unitarian choir to sing the song "Siyahamba." Our choir stood in front of the San Francisco choir and began to sing the words of the song in Zulu. We sang the song through one time. The melody reminded me of what a small choir of angels might make high in the hills of Austria. There was a small pause and a quite hush came over the audience. We started singing the first few notes of the song again and suddenly were joined by what sounded like the Mormon Tabernacle choir singing the notes along with us.

The music sounded heavenly, and the spirit of love and connection filled the room. We sang the song through three times and then asked the audience to sing along with us for the last time. When we all finished singing tears swelled in the eyes of us all. We had been a part of making music that day and we had honored an African musical song. It was an amazing experience for all who were present. I truly felt the spirit of South African music. I had an entirely new appreciation for the rich musical history that plays such an important part of the culture.

CHAPTER SEVEN:
THE LAND, THE PLACE,
THE BEAUTY

I can remember the first time I looked out upon the Atlantic Ocean from the shores of Cape Town, South Africa. I have been to both the Atlantic and Pacific Ocean shores and looked out from various beaches, but nothing compared to the majesty I saw that morning. It was high tide, so the waves were roaring towards the rocky shore. I watched the waves come in and out and was amazed at the quiet sounds that they made as they rushed against the rocks. Sandy beaches in Cape Town do exist but not in the area where I was standing that morning. I gazed out into the horizon and there I saw the outline of a barge perhaps headed to Europe or the other way to the Far East.

Birds flew overhead and made the gnawing sound that gulls make in America. They seemed to hover above the water and then as if they knew where the fish were, they would dive down and capture a creature in their bills and fly back up into the sky.

That morning I enjoyed my solitude while standing and watching this wonderful creation of nature as the water rose and lowered and continued its movement. Far down on the beach, I noticed a mother and child. The child seemed to chase the waves as they rolled in. The mom sat back with bravery and allowed her young child to experience the moment.

The longer I stood looking out the waves I felt a calming effect upon my very nature. I heard music in the constant rhythm of the waves. The water, the waves, and the sounds all combined as if to act as a symphony for me to enjoy as I watched and observed this peaceful-sounding world.

The Sun was up, and its shadow of pink and orange hues cast a beautiful reflection across the water. Many of the fears of ministry around failure, finances and meeting the congregation's expectations seemed to melt away as I stood and observed this unusual, majestic site of nature and all her wonder. Throughout my stay in Cape Town, this spot became my refuge of peace and calm. When I felt alone, frustrated, and at times questioned why I was here, I would come to this place and within minutes my troubles seemed to wash away with the rhythm of the tides.

Cape Town is a beautiful city that sits around the base of a mountain as a backdrop and the ocean as a front room. Its unique history goes back to the Early Dutch who found the area to be a great place to plant tea.

The area known today as Cape Town means "where clouds gather".[39] The first Europeans to discover the Cape were the Portuguese. Bartholomeu Dias arrived in 1488 after journeying South along the West coast of Africa. The next recorded European sighting of the Cape was by Vasco da Gama in 1497 while he was searching for a route that would lead directly from Europe to Asia.[40]

---

[39]Worden, Nigel; van Hyningen, Elizabeth; Bickford-Smith, Vivian (1998). *Cape Town: The Making of a City*. Claremont, Cape Town, South Africa: David Philip Publishers.
[40]*"Vasco da Gama | Biography, Achievements, Route, Map, Significance, & Facts"*. *Encyclopedia Britannica*.

One of the real jewels of the city of Cape Town is a large plateau called Table Mountain. It is practically impossible to find a spot in Cape Town that is not in the shadow of Table Mountain; this majestic plateau dominates the city's skyline and makes a photogenic backdrop to virtually any picture. But people don't just gaze upon it; you can scale the stately 3,500-foot-tall behemoth in many ways. Hiking trails range from challenging to near death-defying, or, if you're the more easy-going type, you can take the cable car up and down in five minutes flat each way.

I, being the adventurous type, but also easy-going, chose to take the cable car ride to the top of the mountain. What awaited me at the top was a vista that took my breath away. From my vantage point I was able to take in the view of the City of Cape Town with its ocean and beaches on one side, and the rock formation, Lion's Head, and skyscrapers on the other. Off in the distance was a great view of Robben Island.

Navigating the various paths on the mesa's flat top allowed me to take in a different view at every turn. Along my paths I saw plenty of unique plant life that make up the Cape's distinctive fynbos vegetation. From a distance, fynbos vegetation appears to be unimpressive but up close it a mosaic of flora bursting with flowers every month of the year. Proteas are the most famous flower that can be found in many forms and on the edges of Table Mountain and other rock formations.

While on top of the mountain I decided to veer off the paths. I wanted to get away from the crowds and enjoy a peaceful moment on the mountain peak. I found a trail that led me away from the main area and within five minutes I found a rock formation and stood upon it and looked out at a view of green vegetation. In the distance it appeared that the top of the plateau of Table Mountain was reaching up to touch the blue sky. A sense of wonder filled my soul and I felt as if I was in touch with a place where time stood still. I felt as if I was one with the beauty of nature which jumped out all around me.

Another part of the City of Cape Town where I found refuge is an area called The Company's Garden[41], which is the oldest garden in South Africa. The garden was originally created in the 1650s by the region's first European

41 ?

settlers and provided fertile ground to grow fresh produce to replenish ships rounding the Cape.[42]

The Dutch East India Company established the garden in Cape Town to provide fresh vegetables to the settlement as well as passing ships. Master gardener, Hendrik Boom, prepared the first ground for the sowing of seed on 29 April 1652. The settlers sowed different kinds of seeds and kept records thereof each day. Through trial and error, they managed to compile a calendar which they used for the sowing and harvesting throughout the year. At first, they grew salad herbs, peas, large beans, radish, beet, spinach, wheat, cabbage, asparagus and turnips, among others.

By 1653 the garden allowed the settlers to become self-sustainable throughout the year. By 1658 nearly every garden plant of Europe and India was already cultivated in the garden. During the 17th century, the garden was made famous by writers of various nationalities, claiming that visitors who had seen the most celebrated gardens of Europe and India agreed that nowhere else in the world was there so great a variety of trees and shrubs of vegetables and flowers blended together.

Today the gardens are a central gathering place; many times, on a warm spring or summer day one can find individuals sitting on the vast lawns with their picnics and enjoying the beauty of the day and the grounds. I loved to go walking in the gardens and always found my walks to be both reflective and peaceful. The gardens stand today as a reminder of the perseverance and resilience of earlier settlers who came to Cape Town to chart out a new life for themselves.

There is little in the world more calming for me than strolling in an immaculate garden. It does not matter where the garden is, who the garden belongs to and how it got there; the most important fact is that walking around in nature can soothe my soul like nothing else on Earth. When I discovered Kirstenbosch,

---

[42] *"Company Gardens Cape Town". South African Heritage Resource Agency. Archived from the original on 23 August 2013. Retrieved 1 September 2012.*

[423] *"Van Riebeecks Hedge Kirstenbosch Botanical". South African Heritage Resource Agency. Archived from the original on 26 April 2012. Retrieved 28 November 2011.*

a botanical garden nestled at the eastern foot of Table Mountain, I felt that I had found one of the most peaceful places on earth.[43]

Kirstenbosch places a strong emphasis on the cultivation of indigenous plants. When Kirstenbosch was founded in 1913 to preserve the flora native to South Africa's territory, it was the first botanical garden in the world with this esthetic, at a time when invasive species were not considered an ecological and environmental problem.

The garden includes a large Conservatory (The Botanical Society Conservatory) exhibiting plants from many different regions, including savanna, fynbos, karoo and others. Outdoors, the focus is on plants native to the Cape region, highlighted by the spectacular collections of proteas.

Kirstenbosch National Botanical Garden claims to be one of the best botanical gardens in the world, and in my personal experience, that statement rings very true. The people who work in the garden, along with the people who visit, all develop a love and respect for the work that this conservation initiative does; they preserve plants from all over the world for the public's viewing and enjoyment.

One of the most colorful neighborhoods in the city of Cape Town is an area called Bo Kemp. Bo Kemp was settled in the late 18th century by Malaysians who had been brought into the cape area to help work the land. They brought with them their religious traditions and beliefs which were Muslim. They had settled in this part of the city which was well known for its bright-colored houses and its strong and dedicated Muslim population.[44]

When you walk the streets of Bo Kemp, it is as if you had taken a step back in time. Some dwellings are small but have been painted in various bright, exciting colors. The history behind the brightly colored dwellings was that when the Malaysians were brought over, these were their homes and the overseers insisted that these only be painted white. When they gained their independence, they chose to paint over the white dwellings in as many bright colors as they could.

While serving as the minister to the Cape Town Unitarian congregation, I became involved with a movement that was set up to preserve the area known as Bo Kemp. Developers were anxious to develop and build high-rise housing

---

[44]Townsend, Lesley (2015-10-15). "History and Style of the Bo-Kaap". *The Heritage Portal*. The Heritage Portal. Retrieved 2018-05-30.

on the hills of Bo Kemp which would not only destroy housing stock but have an environmental effect upon the area.

The developers were proposing that a high rise be built on a hill that looked down on the Muslim cemetery. The cemetery had been there since the late 18th century and the high-rise construction would require digging up the cemetery to install drainage for the complex.[45]

The leader of the Muslims came to the faith community in Cape Town and asked for help in fighting the city and the developers. The faith community came together to save the cemetery and to save the uniqueness of the area called Bo Kemp for the many visitors to enjoy.

It is said that there is strength in numbers. Fifteen different faith communities came together at a Cape Town City Planning commission meeting and shared their concerns that the Planning commission is denied the permits to the developers. The area known as Bo Kemp was preserved and the Muslim area cemetery was saved from demolition.

South Africa is not a third-world country and is very advanced in its technologies and its leadership in the world. One can never forget that clear back in 1965 South Africa was famous for the first successful heart transplant. Innovation in medicine, wine production, banking, and technology continue today to help form a thriving South African economy.

My time in Cape Town was a great education for me. I connected with the history, the beautiful sounds and sites of nature, the culture, and its people. The land, the history of the land, and the resilience of the South African people are a testimony of the power of ideas and how a group of dedicated leaders can bring about change that makes a lasting contribution to the generations that follow.

---

[45]**The Tana Baru Cemetery** is a Muslim cemetery where some of the earliest and respected Muslim settlers of South Africa were buried. The cemetery is located in Bo-kaap, Cape Town. "History of the Tana Baru at a Glance". Tana Baru. Archived from the original on 9 August 2013. Retrieved 1 October 2014.

CHAPTER EIGHT:
A HISTORY OF UNITARIANS IN SOUTH AFRICA

The Unitarian Church has a long history in the country of South Africa. The Unitarian movement in South Africa was founded in 1867 by the Reverend David Faure, member of a well-known Cape family. He encountered advanced liberal religious thought while completing his studies at the University of Leiden in Holland for the ministry of the Dutch Reformed Church in Cape Town.[46]

On his return to South Africa, he preached a probationary sermon in the Groote Kerk, one of the most famous buildings in Cape Town. This led to a public appeal for him to find a community based upon what was called the

---

[46]"Rev David Faure". *faure.co.za.* Retrieved 9 October 2018.

"new theology." The new theology as preached by David Faure was grounded in what he described as "the very essence of religion" — Love of God and love of neighbor.

The state church at the time was the Dutch Reformed Church. The Reverend David Faure had studied and attended seminary in England hoping to come back to South Africa and lead a congregation. Part of his final ministry training was to preach a sermon before the Ministerial Governing Board from the Dutch Reformed who would decide his fate and either grant him his minister credentials or not.

Responding to popular appeal, David Faure gathered a congregation of people who felt the need for a church unfettered by traditional dogmas, open to the advances of modern knowledge and receptive to new spiritual insights.

Reverend Faure preached about a free and unifying religion where men could choose to state how they believed. He further went on to explain that everyone has worth, and it was our responsibility to see the inherent value and dignity in all people. He spoke of a free quest for truth — that everyone had the capacity to choose and follow their truths that best represented what they choose to believe.

When he finished his sermon, the crowd cheered — all except the Governing Board from the Dutch Reformed Church. Angry and upset, they said such talk was not worthy or becoming for a Dutch Reformed Minister. As a result, he would not be given his credentials and was asked to leave the church. So Faure left that day and took a small group of about 30 individuals who had gathered to support him.

Together, they formed the Free Protestant Church of Cape Town. Four years later, Faure learned of Unitarianism and wrote to England and asked if he and his congregation could convert to a Unitarian congregation. They were granted permission and the Church became known as the Unitarian Church of Cape Town. Between 1867 to 1890 the fledgling church, known as the Free Protestant Church, rented space in a commercial building in Cape Town, and in 1890 a warehouse was purchased and converted into the present church. The church today is still using that same building. While a lot has happened over the past 150 years, for the most part the Unitarian church has stood as a symbol of truth and freedom — a place where all are welcomed regardless of their race, creed or nationality.[47]

Rev Faure continued as minister until 1897 at which time he was succeeded by Rev Ramsden Balmforth, from England. He conducted a thriving ministry to 1937 and brought the Free Protestant Church into the international Unitarian Movement in 1921. He ushered the church into the next century and saw a growth of the congregation. As the church was expanding, South Africa was growing as well. In 1911, South Africa had become a free and independent state from England.

Ministers who followed Balmforth were William and Wilma Constable (1937-1941), Donald Livingstone (1941-1949), Magnus Ratter (1949-1960 and 1971-1976), Victor Carpenter (1962-1967), Eugene Widrick (1968-1971), Leon Fay (1977-1979), Robert Steyn (1979-1997).[48]

When I arrived in Cape Town and walked into the sanctuary for the first time, I stood in awe of the rich history that had transpired in that building. I thought about all those ministers who had gone before me and contemplated the challenges they must have dealt with and the many experiences they had. Even though I knew I had big shoes to fill, standing there in that moment I was excited for the calling to lead this congregation through their next journey of discovery.

With great enthusiasm, I ventured to the national archives in Cape Town to research all the ministers who preached before me and it there that I discovered their preserved stories and sermons. Through reading these historical documents, I became intimately familiar with their work. I learned the Reverend Victor Carpenter, for example, had served the Cape Town congregation during the 1960s — a turbulent time in the congregation and in South Africa. Apartheid was in full force and the opposition was strong. The Reverend Carpenter had opened the church to all people regardless of their nationality or race by standing in direct opposition to the law of the land. Nevertheless, he felt strongly that it was crucial for the people of Cape Town to be allowed the

---

[47]Oliver, G. "Unitarian history — South Africa". *unitarian.co.za*. Retrieved 9 October 2018.
[49]Heller-Wagner, Eric (1995). "Radical religion and civil society: The Unitarians of South Africa" (PDF). In De Gruchy, John W.; Martin, S. (eds.). *Religion and the reconstruction of civil society*. Pretoria: University of South Africa.

opportunity to gather in a religious community where they could be welcomed and accepted.

Reverend Carpenter became a staunch supporter of the resistance movement. He even transported cash that was being contributed by those who also opposed the apartheid government and its policies of segregation. On one of his many trips to England, he was asked if he could transport over 30,000 pounds from England back to the resistance in South Africa. The money had come from the UUA service committee — money that was donated from Unitarians all around the world.

With great personal risk, Reverend Carpenter agreed to transport the funds with the knowledge that if he were caught, he and his family could be deported, just one of many possible ramifications. He put the money in the bottom of one side of his suitcase and sent his wife out to purchase a vast number of pink slippers. He put brown paper over the money and carefully placed the pink slippers on top.

He boarded a plane to Johannesburg, South Africa, where upon arrival, he was detained at customs. The customs officer opened his luggage and saw the pink slippers. He asked the reverend what he does with all the slippers. The reverend, without missing a beat responded, "I like to smell them". The guard rolled his eyes and let the reverend pass, never searching for what was underneath the slippers. The funds were successfully delivered to the resistance and Reverend Carpenter was able to continue to fulfill the needs of his congregation and the community of which he and his family were a part.[49]

Other ministers, such as Bob Steyn, served for well over 45 years. Each minister was called by the congregation and left a mark upon the history of the church and the area of Cape Town. Reverend Steyn was known for always providing a sack lunch on Wednesday for the homeless. Those in the community knew that each Wednesday they could stop by the Unitarian church and a meal would be waiting for them.

Reverend Steyn was well known in the community as a leader of truth, and someone who was always standing up for those who were less fortunate. As a result, the Unitarian church swelled in membership. with many families

---

[49] 2011 Annual Award for Distinguished Service to the Cause of Unitarian Universalism: Rev. Victor H. Carpenter, History of South Africa Unitarians.

joining and becoming active participants in the growing, changing community. The church and the building became a gathering place for concerts, discussions, and a place where individuals could congregate to share their beliefs freely without fear of retributions.

Upon Reverend Steyn's sudden death, the congregation was left without a minister. Gordon Oliver had known Reverend Steyn while working as the mayor of Cape Town and decided he would like to lead the congregation. The next few months he attended training in England and later that year because the next minister of the Cape Town Unitarian Congregation.

Reverend Oliver led the church at a time when the nation of South Africa was changing. Nelson Mandela had been released from prison. apartheid had been abolished, and the country was headed for its first free democratic elections. There was a spirit of excitement throughout the country which was echoed in the congregation. Many families and particularly people of color could now experience a life free from government oppression.

Under Reverend Oliver's leadership, branches of the Cape Town Church were formed in Somerset West, Johannesburg, and Durban. Unitarianism was expanding into other parts of South Africa, and it was an exciting time to watch the unique growth that was occurring. Many South Africans were looking for a place in which they could form a community, and the Cape Town Unitarian church provided just such a venue.

Families looking for a place to raise their children with strong liberal religious beliefs joined the Cape Town Unitarian church. Longtime members welcomed the newcomers, and this became an exciting time for new ideas and new ways of looking at many of the traditions of the past.

Reverend Oliver retired after many years and Reverend Roux was called to serve. He had recently joined the church and had been trained as a Dutch Reformed Minister. While he worked hard for eight years, he eventually found that it was time to step aside. It was at this point that the congregation decided that they needed to search for someone from outside of the norm to come in and help them to determine how they could move forward. They started looking for an interim minister, and to my great good fortune, I was contacted and offered that opportunity.

The Cape Town Church has a membership of approximately 100 people, of whom about 50 are regular church attendees. In the past, the church had called ministers from America to serve but I was the first one for well over 30 years. The congregation needed leadership as well as an understanding of what the role of a minister entailed. I knew that if I were to be successful, I needed to lead by teaching, as well as establishing full transparency. Therefore, each week I would send out my schedule to all the members and friends of the congregation.

Gradually, the congregation came to trust me; together we worked on identifying their vision and goals for the next year, three years, and five years. Some members were interested in learning more about worship and sermon writing. A class was held for eight weeks with 10 attendees. The results were that each member wrote a sermon and came to understand the arc of worship and all the things that go into executing an engaging worship experience.

These members went on to preach and oversee different worship services and felt that they were better trained to handle lay worship. It was an exciting experience for me to watch each of them grow and develop in their understanding as well as in their delivery of their written ideas. This class was one of many minister experiences that I will always cherish. These participants taught me that when members are encouraged to pursue their worship ideas, good things can happen. As a result, two members decided to pursue full time ministry and are preparing to enter the seminary to be trained, something that gave me great joy.

The church has grown in recent years. 11 new members have been registered in the last two years and regular "Build Your Own Theology" programs for interested persons who are not Unitarians have been held; some of them have become members or attended church from time to time. The Church provides a service to non-churchgoing couples who come for marriage counseling, to have children blessed, or the conduction of memorial services.

South Africa has Unitarian Congregations in Somerset West, Johannesburg, and Durban. Each of these fellowships were formed by members who because of work and other circumstances left the Cape Town Unitarian Church and formed three fellowships. The fellowships are still active today.50

Somerset West Unitarians

Since 1984 there has been an active fellowship in Somerset West, which is about 40 kilometres outside Cape Town. Their meetings are held in a private home and conducted in the form of a discussion with readings and prayer.

Johannesburg Unitarian Fellowship

In the 1950s the Johannesburg Fellowship was started by Reverend Donald Livingstone with the help of Unitarian minister, Margaret Barr, who worked with the Unitarians of the Khasi Hills in India for many years. She visited South Africa in the 1950s and was invited by Livingstone to address a meeting of interested persons in Johannesburg. This Fellowship has remained active since then and meets monthly.

The Durban Congregation

The Durban Congregation has been active since 1986 and meets twice monthly in Westville. Durban Unitarians often comment that they attend services because they 'enjoy them so much', not because they feel they 'ought to'.

My Involvement: While serving in Cape Town as the unitarian minister, I had the opportunity to preach at the Summerset West Unitarian Fellowship, lead a Zoom call with the Johannesburg Unitarian Fellowship and spoke with the Durban Unitarian Fellowship. All fellowships are active today and meet on a regular schedule.

A qualified and vetted minister became the interim minister. She had been trained in the Unity church but had embraced Unitarianism and understood the power of ministry and the calling of a minister. She leads the Cape Town Congregation today carrying out many of the traditions from the past and is developing and forming new traditions for the future.

I often reflect upon that first moment when I stood and stared at the back wall of the church building. On that wall were photos of past ministers the Cape Town Unitarian Church. I remember my feelings at that time were ones

---

50"The Unitarians of South Africa — A Socio-historical Study" doctoral thesis of Rev Eric Heller-Wagner, an American Unitarian Universalist, now minister in Sydney, Australia, who visited Cape Town in the early 1990s to complete his doctorate at the University of Stellenbosch

of wonderment and awe. My time spent with the Cape Town Unitarian as their minister will always hold a place of comfort and joy in my heart. I can't help but feel and believe that the future of Unitarianism is in good hands. The Cape Town church has a well-developed and trained lay leadership team and they are helping to lead the church into the next chapter.

CHAPTER 9:
GRIEF AND LOSS

Here in America and much of Canada, we have memorial traditions that have stood the test of time for decades, even centuries. But our end-of-life traditions are vastly different from those in other countries and cultures. Such was the case that I found in South Africa. The customs vary depending upon the person and their beliefs but understanding and processing grief in South Africa is a vastly different approach than in Western societies.[51]

In Western societies, one learns of death in the abstract, so to speak. The knowledge of death is cerebral; neither the heart nor the eye experiences it directly. When death does occur, the dying and their loved ones are too often

---

[51]Front. Psychol., 24 September 2021 | https://doi.org/10.3389/fpsyg.2021.604987

segregated, left stranded alone for what is, after all, the second most profound experience in a human being's life.

Today, in America, death as a natural experience has been removed from most Americans' lives. There is no witnessing of the birth/death cycle as it would have been in our country even less than 100 years ago. There is less connection with others and few rituals to guide behavior.

In addition, our society excludes the aged and sick from our day-to-day lives. When our older relatives become frail, it has become the norm to find care in professional residential settings, or nursing homes. This makes the dying process foreign, something that we do not witness directly, or incorporate into our daily lives.

In the United States, there are few rituals associated with grieving, and the handling of the body after death is turned over to paid professionals, from the efficient and sterile way in which the nurses are trained to handle the body from the time of death to the way the morticians prepare the body with cosmetics, hair styling, and clothing to give it the appearance of life. The funeral directors, undertakers, morticians, and other paid professionals all work together to keep the "messiness" of death away from us.

Western cultures tend to view death as a feared enemy that can be defeated by modern medicine and fancy high-tech machines. Our language reflects this battle mentality. We say that people "combat illness" or "fall victim" to illness after a "long struggle." And we use euphemistic language to describe death, such as s/he is "no longer with us" or has "passed on."

This is not the case in South Africa. The night preceding a South African funeral service, a vigil is usually held in the home of the deceased until the morning. Pictures, mirrors, and other reflective surfaces are turned over or covered. The deceased's bed is also removed from their room. Family, friends, and community members can attend and pay their respects to the deceased. It is a time to comfort the family of the loss of their loved one.[52] Interestingly, a ritual killing of an animal for the ancestors is sometimes done to prevent any more misfortunes from occurring in the family.[53]

---

[51]Cultural Spotlight: South African Funeral Traditions by Jenny Goldade; Jan. 27, 2017

[52]The bellowing of a bull before a ritual slaughter is a joyous sign to many South Africans that their ancestors have accepted the animal's sacrifice. Thousands of animals are killed every month in South Africa in tribal cleansing ceremonies, and rituals marking births, deaths and weddings. ... Feb 9, 2007 LATIMES

A South African funeral service is a place for celebrating and mourning the deceased. The life history is shared and many times friends, family members, and even sometimes siblings share their remembrances at the funeral service.

For the burial, the deceased may be wrapped in slaughtered animal skin, or buried with personal items, such as food, clothes, kitchen utensils, or blankets. Some people may choose cremation, but it's not accepted in certain religions, like Judaism. After the funeral service is over, everyone is welcomed back to the deceased's home for a meal and a continued celebration of the deceased's life.

The formal mourning period can last at least a week after the funeral service. During this time, mourners may not socialize or leave their house, must refrain from loud talking or laughing, wear black, and shave their hair to symbolize death and new life. Widows remain in mourning for at least a year. Creating a memorial tradition to honor the deceased, such as visiting the gravesite, can help mourners heal.

These types of rituals can help the family and individual to process their grief and begin to move on. Grief can come into each of our lives in different ways. It isn't always associated with the loss of a loved one. Sometimes it shows up in those situations where we are faced with changes in our lives and our relationships. Such was the case for me as I came face to face with a different type of grief, one not related to the loss of a loved one but to face dealing with a change in my daily relationship.

South Africans take comfort and pride in the way they choose to grieve, and honor departed loved ones. When thinking about this book and the various ideas I wished to convey, I felt strongly that a chapter about grief and loss would be important to talk about. I experienced grief and loss in my life with serving as a minister in South Africa. It wasn't the type of grief/loss that hits one when a family member, friend, or colleague dies. It was the grief that occurs when we come face to face with change. In my case, it was thrust upon me because of my change in residence and who I lived with.

When I first arrived in South Africa, my partner Jerry was with me and we experienced the joy that comes from seeing places, meeting people, and enjoying new experiences for the first time together. In the month that he was with me we went to all the tourist attractions, went to dinner with members of the Unitarian congregation, and just spent quiet moments walking along the beach or hiking in the hills. These experiences helped us both to experience this new land of South Africa in ways that helped set a solid foundation for the rest of my time there.

I still remember standing at Cape Town International Airport and trying to say goodbye to Jerry knowing that it would be at least six more months before we would be reunited. As I held him and looked into his eyes, I realized that once he left, I would be on my own. We said goodbye with tears in our eyes, and I watched him walk away and go through security and disappear into the vastness of Cape Town Airport.

On the drive back to my house I was struck with the realization that now my success or failure here in South Africa was fully dependent upon me. Jerry had left and even though we would talk regularly, the minutes and hours of each day depended upon me. For much of my adult life, I have had to learn how to be reliant upon myself for my success and this experience was no different.

As those first days and weeks rolled by, I had very little time to think about being alone. When the days started to wind down and I found myself alone in my home, that was when the loss of not having my partner with me hit. Not having someone to talk to, share my day with and just be present with took a lot of getting used to.

At the time I didn't look upon my feelings and thoughts during those quiet moments as those of grief. However, now that I look back upon that time with objectivity, I can see now that I was grieving. That is the interesting thing about grief — it comes knocking on the door many times uninvited and with full force that at times can be very debilitating.

For some this debilitating feeling can wash over the grieving party to the extent that they find it hard to function and to have hope. For others, this type of grief comes as a wave that they have learned how to sit with and let pass. No matter how grief is experienced, it is part of the healing process which I believe comes from being able to acknowledge the grief that one is feeling. Such was the case in my situation.

Here I was in a strange country with my friends and family over 8,400 miles away. My closest Minister Unitarian colleague was 3,500 miles away. I was the only fully ordained Unitarian Universalist minister on the entire continent of Africa! The grief that I experienced was that feeling of being all alone and the loss of having those that I had depended upon for support so very far away from me.

At times my grief and loss felt like I was all alone and that if I just stayed busy, I would not have to sit with the feelings I was experiencing. My days became full and I would make sure that each moment was filled with meetings with members, community colleagues, and other interfaith ministers. I found that if my day was kept busy with doing that, I would be too tired at night to face the grief and loss I was experiencing.

This is the thing about grief, it doesn't just go away. The busier I got the more and more I made sure that I didn't have to face the feelings I was experiencing. One day I had had enough. I arose early, drove to one of my favorite places, parked the car, and began to walk along the beach. With the backdrop of the Atlantic Ocean to the side of me, I could hear the roar of the waves crashing upon the shore and receding out.

I thought about my life, my family, my friends, and where I was at. My emotions got the best of me and I started to cry. As the tears flowed, I felt a release of emotions and feelings and I realized there was a part of me that was missing my former life — my friends, my family, and all those things that were familiar to me.

I also realized that things continually change and that in our lives they are always in a flux of transformation. The more I walked along the beach I realized that the feelings I had been experiencing were attached to the grief that I was facing. The loss that I felt of my ordinary world-changing and the uncertainty of having to create a new world, a new reality, and a new way of being.

I wondered how many times in each of our lives we come face to face with the power of change in our lives. Perhaps it is a change of jobs, loss of a friend, loss of a family member, or just plain loss of the simple things in our lives.

Grieving is a personal experience. Depending on who you are and the nature of your loss, your process of grieving will be different for everyone. There is no "normal and expected" period of time for grieving. Some people adjust to a new life within several weeks or months. Others take a year or more, particularly when their daily life has been radically changed or their loss was traumatic and unexpected.

I found the process by which the South Africans handle grief and loss very comforting. Although it may be possible to postpone grieving, it is not possible to avoid grieving altogether. If life circumstances make it difficult for you to stop, feel, and live through the grieving process, you can expect grief to eventually erupt sometime in the future. In the meantime, unresolved grief can affect your quality of life and relationships with others.

Grief is a normal part of life and is experienced by most of us at some point. People deal with grief in various ways, and there is no prescribed path or predictable group of stages that must be followed. "The Stages of Grief" by Elizabeth Kubler-Ross has proven to be a helpful guide. She describes the five stages as 1) Denial and Isolation, 2) Anger, 3) Bargaining, 4) Depression and Sadness, and 5) Acceptance. It is important to remember, though, that people process grief in their own way and in their own time. Some people prefer to grieve alone, while others prefer to be surrounded by others.[54]

I found that by staying busy and surrounding myself with others, I was able to process the grief that I felt concerning the daily physical absence of my partner. Jerry and I learned how to survive and how to manage a long-distance relationship and still stay connected. Part of the key was for both of us to acknowledge the grief that we felt about being separated but at the same time look for ways each day that we could honor and support each other. One of the most impactful things we did each day was have a live phone conversation with each other.

I hope that as you deal with grief and loss in your life that you will be able to take strength from some of the practices, rituals and methods that are practiced in South Africa. I found great comfort in the rituals around death and life. I also learned a lot more about grief and the importance of sitting and allowing

---

[54]Five Stages of Grief; Elizabeth Kubler-Ross Banner; 2018

oneself to be in the moment with those feelings. I learned a lot about the grief process as I worked with members of my Unitarian congregation. My partner and I have a stronger relationship today because of our separation. We both have learned the importance of staying engaged with others, reaching out when needed, and sharing with people what you need at the time.

All of us will experience several types of grief in our lifetime. I have come to understand that everyone chooses to handle their grief in a variety of ways. For some, they shut down and spend time being alone with themselves and closing themselves off to others and the world around them.

Recognizing our grief and how our grief journeys are different is important for our well-being. You may feel the pressure to move on from your loss, but I believe it is essential that you permit yourself to take your time with your grief process so that you may experience healthy outcomes.

Some of you might view ongoing grief as a personal failure or a sign of weakness. It is not. In my work as a minister, in working with grieving members of my community, I have learned how some compartmentalize their grief to get through the burdens of tasks expected of them. This can be a great coping mechanism but may not be helpful if someone is burying or hiding from their grief. I believe that when we recognize and validate our ongoing grief, we can begin to understand it as a part of ourselves rather than apart from ourselves.

Early on in my ministry, while serving as a chaplain, I was called upon each day to offer comfort and support to individuals, families, and others who were dealing with a loss of a loved one. Most of the time these families and individuals just wanted to talk to me about their loved ones. I learned a great deal about how to offer what is known as "Ministry of Presence"— by being fully present and by active listening — in other words, by simply allowing them to be with the full range of their emotions.

My chaplaincy experience taught me that it can be hard to understand the shape and weight of one's grief, especially when they are juggling expectations from work, family, and friends. I witnessed that one day a person experiencing grief may feel hopeful regarding their future and the next day feel despair over the loss or losses that they are experiencing.

As a minister and as a chaplain I find it important to understand the grief I might be feeling at any given time and to check with myself and identify the emotions that I am feeling concerning the loss. In council with my community, I've learned how important it is to take the time to sit with your grief and consider the emotions and the impact that the loss has had on your life. I recommend some self-talk to validate one's feelings and how they affect you.

Consider journaling and capturing your thoughts, feelings and ideas, and attitudes. I have found that writing can have a very healing and settling effect. I have also learned that when I make time to journal, emotions, and thoughts that are spiraling in my head doesn't seem so overwhelming.

Learn how to actively remember your loved one. Develop or engage in a purposeful remembrance of them. Consider ways to incorporate memories of your loved one into your daily life. I lost a very close friend a few years ago and this friend loved colored cut glass. I have a piece that belonged to her and I keep it on my desk. Each day I am reminded of the joy and love that she brought into my life.

Lastly, identify and use a support system. It can be beneficial to talk through your grief to understand and make sense of your losses and your emotional responses over time. Always seek out friends, family, or professionals who will empathically listen to and support you.

The role of hope in the grief process can also help us to cultivate resilience, gratitude, and love. I cannot underestimate the practice of cultivating optimism. Optimism may seem daunting when amid grief, but I believe it is through actively maintaining a positive outlook that we begin to see a future in which we feel gratitude for the supportive people in our lives and those moments of love, laughter, and joy that lie ahead.

CHAPTER TEN:
WHAT IS THE FUTURE OF
UNITARIANISM IN AFRICA

Unitarianism has had a colorful history in Africa. The Movement has been in Africa since 1867, when a young Dutch Reformed minister, the Reverend David Faure, a member of a well-known Cape Town family, founded the church.[55] Reverend Faure encountered advanced liberal religious thought while completing his studies at the University of Leiden in Holland for the ministry of the Dutch Reformed Church in Cape Town.

Unitarianism in Africa is anything but uniform in history and tradition. Africa is a place that, before European colonization, was a collection of very

---

[55]Heller-Wagner, Eric (1995). "Radical religion and civil society: The Unitarians of South Africa"

local cultures, tribes, and economies. That history infuses the African continent today. Wars are often tribally and ethnically charged, as are politics, dress, and culture. Improved transportation and the expansion of mobile phone accessibility have started to expand the worldview in many African countries, especially in the cities, but the ties of tradition are still strong.

Unitarianism in Burundi, Uganda, Congo, and Kenya is pretty much brand new. In Bujumbura, Burundi, Fulgence Ndagijimana was a fallen-away Catholic seminarian. In 2003 he found Unitarianism on the internet, contacted an English minister, and on his advice gathered his own church.[56]

Since 2004, Fulgence has quietly gathered a community of 25 like-minded people. Their growth is limited by several factors, one of them being a lack of French worship and program resources.

In English-speaking Uganda, Mark Kiyamba also found Unitarianism through the Internet. With no language barrier and relative peace in his nation, Mark has been able to gather a congregation of 150 people in Kampala.[57] But the Ugandan story is even more remarkable. Seeing a need, yet having no resources, no space, and no teachers, they just went ahead and started a congregation and school for children with AIDS in the countryside. Right now, they have 50 members and 450 students.

Congo-Brazzaville is another French-speaking country. Alaiin Yengue is an anthropologist. Unlike other African Unitarians, he did not come from a Christian background, but an animist tradition of ancient tribal religion. In 2005, he was waiting for his brother to get off work in a Brazzaville hotel one day when he struck up a conversation with an American gentleman. They talked about religion and that is when Alaiin learned about Unitarianism. The man suggested that with unitarian liberal views and acceptance of paganism, it might be a bridge from the old world to the new in Congo. Using the internet, Alaiin made a connection with Jean-Claude Barbier, the secretary for Assemblée Fraternelle des Chrétiens Unitariens in France. The group now meets regularly and is looking to grow.[58]

---

[56]Vice President: Fulgence Ndagijimana Archived 2016-12-25 at the Wayback Machine International Council of Unitarians and Universalists

[57]Branch, Gregory (March 5, 2010). "Ugandan activists to petition government to scrap anti-gay bill". The Institute on Religion and Public Policy. Archived from the original on 25 August 2011.

[58]African Unitarianism a sermon by Rev. Brian J. Kiely Unitarian ...April 2008

By far the fastest-growing Unitarian community is in Kenya. It is comprised of four main communities, and all owe their discovery of Unitarianism to Rev. Patrick Magara. Patrick is the only ordained minister in Kenya, although his ordination came from the Seventh Day Adventist tradition. He discovered Unitarianism in 2001 and soon convinced his congregation to follow him into his new faith.[59]

One of the questions that I asked of Unitarians that I met in Africa was, "Why did you become a Unitarian?" Several members from the Cape Town Unitarian Church wanted to share their stories and I have included excerpts from their stories which can be found in "Unitarian Perspectives Reflections from South Africa."

I know each of the individuals and had the opportunity to work with them as their Minister. I found their stories to be very inciteful as to why Africans are choosing to become Unitarians.

Substance in Silence by Shelley Adams[60]
As a ten-year-old child, I engaged in a silent exercise that opened me to a sense of belonging, warmth, and greatness that is the Universe and the nature of who and what I am. At the time, I only had my Catholic religious upbringing to understand and articulate the experience so the best I could do was to say to myself "I am God."

I said this to express to myself that we are all part of and contain the spark of all existence, I had no other way to articulate the wholeness of our existence. Recognizing the heretical nature of this thought but not necessarily of the idea, I buried it and never raised it with anyone.

Over the next ten years, I had interests and experiences and read books that helped to form my personal belief system. As a guiding principle, I understood that my beliefs had to be flexible, changeable, and adaptable to new ideas and truths as they became evident to me. I use the sense of "goodness" as a litmus test to recognize them. And so,

---

[59]The New Church in Kenya by Andrew M. T. Dibb *New Church Life* 113.9 (September 1993): 409–12.
[60]Unitarian Perspectives; Reflections from South Africa; Cape Town Unitarians; Aug 2020 pp10-16

when Cape Town Unitarian sent invitations to participate in a silent retreat, I jumped at the chance.

A few church members and I attended the three-day retreat facilitated by Pat Oliver in October 2014. The weekend consisted of silence from Sunday evening to Tuesday afternoon interspersed with meditation, music, and physical activities.

The experiences I had on the retreat made me realize that we are all connected. I recognized a presence and a rhythm that aligns us all to the Source. This awareness presented itself to me as a visual impression of us all being connected at and from the heart to the beginning and end of all of life.

I chose to become a Unitarian because it allows me to connect with my inner self, with my past, and provides me with insights into my spiritual development.

Belonging or Just Fitting In? by Celeste Esau61

I always felt like an outsider. Dreams and visions as standing on the outside looking in through a window, watching people out in the world living their lives seemingly with ease. I was out in the cold, feeling like an alien, being unable to decipher what was going on or how to fit in. I thought that I was being rejected by my mother and my community because I couldn't be like them. I thought that's what I was supposed to think ... but I didn't.

I felt like I was other and that I just had not found my people yet. Many people have similar experiences of being disillusioned by what is presented as reality and truth. The brave venture to explore the concepts of the here and now in a world that seems to value conformity.

As a little girl, I often would be asked by adults in the community and teachers, "So what do you want to become one day?" and my answer was always 'nothing.' This would upset them, and I wondered how they might have thought I had answered incorrectly or misunderstood the question. I always firmly believed that each of us had been

---

[61]Unitarian Perspectives; Reflections from South Africa; Cape Town Unitarians; Aug 2020 pp 31-33

called to be whoever we need to 'become' anything! Another tradition that I am none too fond of is that of New Year's Resolutions. But I have long since learned that there is value to be found in almost everything. It's usually just a matter of perspective.

My inner wisdom has been my most trusted source for guiding me throughout my life. It has provided me with peace and joy and love beyond all comprehension. It has kept me reliant on no one but the only source of all things (referred to by some people as God, Spirit, Nature, etc.) and encourages me to continue this journey of questioning and listening carefully for the answers that lie deep within.

How exciting it was for me when I found the Cape Town Unitarian (CTU) community. From the moment I stepped into the sanctuary, I knew that it was a welcoming place, beckoning me to explore further and step fully into myself. I enjoyed the service and the music and the fellowship, but what caught my attention was a colorful poster on the wall listing the Seven Unitarian Universalist (UU) Sources. The very first one really stood out and caught my attention.

I quote: "Direct experience of that transcending mystery and wonder, affirmed in all cultures, which moves us to a renewal of the spirit and an openness to the forces which create and uphold life."

That sold me. I knew that I had finally found a place where people seem to be practicing or at least striving towards direct experience and acknowledging it as a connection to the source. When I then saw the poster with the Seven UU Principles that Unitarians strive towards, it was further confirmation for me that this was the place I needed to be.

The Seven Principles start with the inherent worth and dignity of every person (I thought, really? Even me?), and encircling all of that was respect for the interdependent web of all existence, of which we are apart. And I thought, YES!! Connecting with the One and being one with the oneness, acknowledging that we are all inherently worthy and a part of each other … connected to Source … and therefore our direct experience helps us to transcend the mystery of this world.

The Wisdom of Africa, Christianity & Unitarianism Reimagining What A Community of Faith Can Be in Africa by Roux Malan[62]

"Unitarianism has a small footprint in Africa when compared to other faith-based communities. It is also relatively new compared to the longstanding presence of Roman Catholics, Presbyterians, and Methodists on the continent.

Early in the 20th century, a second attempt "at stripping Christianity in Africa of foreign cultural imperialism came about with the establishment of African Indigenous Churches" (Fatokun, 2005). These churches adopted elements of traditional African religion freely to make Christianity relevant to African culture. In South Africa, the Zionist Churches are a good example.

Outside of the religious sphere, much has also been done by African scholars to address burning issues on the African continent, such as African identity, colonialism, racism, and poverty.

In Africa, The Cape Town Unitarian Church is the oldest Unitarian congregation on the continent. Established in 1868 by Rev. David Faure, it has maintained a small, yet resilient community up until the present time. Due to its history and its position within the broader South African society, its church services maintained European values and worldviews.

The first Unitarian church on African soil that made a strong attempt to incorporate the cultural and religious needs of Africans was established by Dr. Bishop Adeniran Adedeji Isola in Lagos, Nigeria, in 1918. The meetings of this new church were conducted in the local Yoruba language and incorporated Yoruba musical instruments such as native drums.

The yearning for a religious community that can embrace African culture and welcome people from different tribes is clearly expressed in the following words of Isaac Choti, a Unitarian in the Kisii district of Kenya:

---

[62]Unitarian Perspectives; Reflections from South Africa; Cape Town Unitarians; Aug 2020 pp25-30

"I had been a Christian all my life, but my church had policies I didn't like. Some churches made it hard for us. They say you can only come with one wife. But Jesus said come as you are. In UU, they welcome everyone."

During my years as full-time minister (2007-2017) of Cape Town Unitarians, I engaged early on with a group of traditional healers in Khayelitsha, one of the townships in Cape Town. In September 2007, I invited them to a celebration of African culture during our weekly Sunday Service. They were delighted and marveled at the ease with which they were accepted at the church.

If Unitarian Churches in Africa wish to find ways to engage emotion and intuition as a valid and essential part of religious and spiritual experience, they need to pay attention to the following key elements: (1) reimagine their church structure and church services. (2) bridge the perceived gap between Christianity and African wisdom. (3) re-discover how to live in-harmony with nature."

I agree with Reverend Roux Malan when he states, "Unitarianism has a small yet significant footprint on the African continent that is growing. As the Unitarian community grows and establishes itself on the continent, it needs to address the issues that other spiritual communities also grapple with, namely indigenization of the faith. To bring this about, Unitarians need to acknowledge the importance of community and feeling within African society and find ways to foster its expression through dancing and singing."

The future of Unitarianism in Africa and South Africa is at a time of potential growth. As countries in Africa take more responsibility for their self-governance, this gives a rise to individual desire to find peace in meaning in their religious expression. Unitarianism is well-posed to offer a sense of community and a place where Africans can connect with their family roots and find a community that is supportive and meaningful. A place where one can feel heard and excepted for who they are and the culture that they come from.

CHAPTER ELEVEN:
ENTERING BACK IN

Departing South Africa was very hard for me. Not only was I leaving people that I had come to love, but I was also leaving behind an enriching experience that had changed my way of thinking and being in the world. In our lives, there are those of us who like to plan and look forward to our vision unfolding seamlessly. This was my hope in preparing to leave South Africa. I had such a wonderful entry into this country and was planning on having a wonderful exit.

Yet life has a way of throwing unforeseen challenges in our path that test our limits, determination, and ultimately our perseverance. Such was the case in my departure from South Africa. I had put things in motion and had been assisting the congregation leadership in assembling a search committee to find their next minister. The committee was meeting regularly and was making progress on developing a packet that would tell the history of the congregation along with its hopes and dreams for the future.

They started an active search. My contract had been extended until March and everything was in place for me to make a successful exit and a well-timed entry back to my life in America. I was feeling very confident in the congregation, in the leadership, and with the work that we had been able to accomplish.

I decided to make a quick trip back to the States to re-apply for an extension on my Visa. In South Africa, the government makes all foreigners apply with the South African Embassy that is closest to their primary residence. Since my home is in Cleveland, that meant I had to work with the embassy in Chicago.

The plan was to leave South Africa, fly back to Chicago, and file my paperwork to extend my stay until the end of March. Many things went wrong in my preparation. For one thing, my leave date kept moving. Trying to arrange my flights back presented another obstacle. After a few days of challenges, I was finally able to secure my itinerary and lodging in Chicago.

On the morning of my departure from Cape Town, I was backing out of my driveway, and lo and behold the gate that went across would not open! I had planned on driving myself to the airport so that I could drop off the rental car. Instead, I had to call an Uber and leave my rental car parked at my place. I wasn't too worried because I knew I would be coming back.

When I got to the airport and went through customs, I was informed that my Visa had expired two days before and that I was now considered an alien and I had overstayed my visit. I was told that I could contact the government authorities but that I would have to leave the country that day. Since I could not go back, I had to board my flight and leave. This was a blow that I had not expected, and I wasn't sure how I was going to solve this. I tried to stay calm, but my emotions were running rampant, and my state of mind was not in the best place. What was I going to do? How was I going to say goodbye? What about my home, my belongings, and the rental car? All these questions ran through my mind repeatedly. I asked for clarity and calmness, but those feelings were elusive.

I soon realized that I couldn't do anything about what has happened until I arrived back in the USA. I told myself to try and just be in the moment and that somehow, I would figure all of this out. I had no idea where the answers would come but I had to have faith that I would receive the clarity I needed to resolve the issues.

After what seemed like hours it was finally time to board my plane. My heart was full as I realized that I had to say goodbye. I somehow felt that all would be made right and that the answers to my questions of what to do would be solved. At that moment, I had to let go and trust the process. I quickly boarded my flight, found my seat, and waited for the plane to depart. Within a half-hour, we were in the air, and I was flying to my first stop which was in the capital city of Ethiopia. Once there I had about thirty minutes to catch my flight to Washington, DC, and then a flight to Chicago.

For the next 10 hours, the plane took me further and further away from South Africa. I was headed home, not the way I had hoped and planned for but headed home, nonetheless. In those quiet moments on the plane, I cried. I worried about my congregation, my friends, and all the people that I had come to love.

The plane landed and I was told to report to the ticket counter because I had missed my flight and had been booked on another flight. This flight was headed to Paris, France where I would have a five and a half hour layover until I could catch my flight to Chicago. When I found all of this out it was 11:30 pm and I had been up for more than 15 hours.

I made my way to my next departure gate knowing that the plane would not be departing until 1:30 a.m. with arrival in Paris, France at 6:30 a.m. The airport was packed as it appeared that many travelers had missed their connecting flights, and everyone seemed upset, just wanting desperately to get out of the airport and on their way. Even amid the throngs of passengers, I felt truly alone.

In my desperation, I noticed a young man who had been on my flight and had sat a few rows behind me. As travelers do in times like this, we struck up a conversation and became fast friends. He was headed back to Washington, DC, and did not like the fact that he had missed his connection. Both of us were seasoned travelers and agreed that the airline owed us an upgrade for the inconvenience they had caused. We asked an airline representative to whom we should talk. She directed us to the customer service desk, but much to our dismay nobody was operating it. We spotted a phone on the desk and called it. We were put in touch with customer service and were told that we would have to go to our assigned gate and talk to the manager on duty.

We quickly made our way to our gate only to find a mass of people on both sides of the gate. They were all trying to depart on planes scheduled to leave within the next hour. It was more than a madhouse — it was a chaotic scene. We finally found a supervisor but were informed that she had no upgrades to offer and that all flights were overbooked.

We reluctantly accepted our situation and were at least grateful to have assigned seats on our flight to Paris. Within a few minutes we were boarding, and our flight took off shortly thereafter. We landed in Paris and spent the next four and a half hours enjoying each other's company at the United flyers club lounge. When it came time for us to depart, we both went our separate ways, never expecting to see each other again.

My time spent with this kind gentlemen had calmed me down considerably; it started to prepare me for the adventure that lie ahead. I landed in Chicago on a Saturday afternoon and realized that I couldn't do anything about my situation until Monday. That would be the soonest I could visit my friend and contact at the South African Embassy. I realized that the most important thing I could do for the remainder of the weekend was to rest my body and mind to get my strength back.

I worried about my congregation, the people, my friends, and my partner Jerry. How was I going to break all of this to him? Finally, on Sunday afternoon I called Jerry and had a conversation. I told him that I would do all that I could here and would let him know how my meeting on Monday worked out.

Monday morning promptly at 9 a.m., I entered the South Africa Embassy Fortunately, I have a friend who works there, and was paired up with her. I showed her my paperwork and then she made some calls to her contacts in South Africa. She asked me to write a letter explaining what had happened and how important it was for the South African government to grant my request to renew my Visa. I quickly wrote the letter while I was in her office. She took what I wrote and emailed it to Internal Affairs in South Africa.

She told me that it would take about two weeks but that all should work out. I left her office and called Jerry and told him of my news. I then found the next available flight out to Cleveland. I arrived in Cleveland that night and thus began another adventure.

The days went by quickly and I never really took the time and energy to settle back in because in my mind I would be going back to South Africa. When I had arrived in the USA, I had picked up this terrible cough and Jerry was concerned and thought that I needed to do something about it. I said that I would but thought that it was due to all my recent air travel.

Meanwhile, I had been communicating with the Council president back in Cape Town. They were getting by without me but were very anxious for me to return. Their search committee had narrowed the minister search down to three prospective candidates. One of those candidates was an internal one and the other two were from the outside. I was pleased to learn that things were progressing on that front.

My cough wasn't getting any better, so I decided to take some over-the-counter medicine to try and get a handle on it. Aside from the cough, I was having terrible headaches. I experienced these on and off since August when I was in Cape Town and had attributed them to stress. I went to the pharmacy and purchased the meds and went home and took them. Within hours my whole body began to swell up.

At first, I thought that perhaps I had put on some extra weight. Jerry came home and voiced his concerns and said that I didn't look right. My stomach was swollen, and my legs and ankles were as well. In addition, I had terrible throbbing headaches and no matter what I took I couldn't get them to reside. I finally relented and agreed with Jerry that I needed to be taken to the hospital emergency room.

Off we went to Metro Hospital and soon I was walking into the hospital emergency room. I was quickly admitted, and the doctors began to take my vitals. I learned that my blood pressure was 185 over 120. This was a possible reason for my headaches. Now the team of medical professionals had to find out for themselves what else was going on.

Test after test was ordered and several scans were done. Finally, after 8 hours of being poked, prodded, and scanned, the team had what they thought were some answers. I was told that I had a growth on my left kidney that was cancerous and that it appeared that my kidney was gone. They scheduled appointments with a kidney doctor and with my urologist. Jerry and I were sent home with scheduled appointments on the following Monday.

We both took the news and cried together and spent a long weekend in much thought and reflection. What would this all mean and how could I possibly go back to South Africa now? It seemed that Monday would never come but finally, it did. There are those times in each of our lives when we connect with the right people at the right time. Such was the case with Dr. Digna, who provided me with the correct information to help me better understand what was going on.

He spent well over 45 minutes asking me questions and going over all my charts. He then informed Jerry and me that my left kidney had stopped operating. Essentially, it had been taken over by cysts that had become active and started growing. The headaches that I had were my body's way of dealing with the loss of the kidney. He also said that the kidney was beyond saving and that I would now have to learn how to survive on one kidney. While I did not have cancer, the growths seen on the scan were cysts that had completely taken over my left kidney. He put me on a medication that I will have to take for the rest of my life and made a return appointment in 60 days.

Jerry and I made our way home feeling relieved but wondering what was next. On our arrival home, I received a call from the South African Embassy. Miraculously, my paperwork had been approved and I would be issued a new visa by the middle of December. At last, a spot of bright news.

Given my health situation, and the fact that during all of this I had been offered a position in Peoria, IL as an interim minister, I decided I would not be returning to South Africa. My new position was to start on February 1st, and it made much more sense to live two states away from Ohio versus an entire continent away. My doctors still had me under advisement and a biopsy of my prostate was scheduled. This was a hard decision but was the right one for me. I shared it with the Cape Town Leadership and the congregation. I had to say goodbye by way of a Zoom meeting and not in person. This was a hard thing for me and them.

Reflecting on my situation, I was so grateful that I was back home in the USA when my illness was discovered and that I had doctors who knew my medical history. It would have been very hard to go through all that I did while living in a foreign country. Not having my partner Jerry around or my friends and family would have been a very difficult situation to endure.

Life often has twists and turns and challenges that we can't always anticipate. I can see the work of the spirit as I look back on what happened to me. I can say that I was where I needed to be and that what happened to me occurred for a reason.

When I accepted the fact that I was not going back to South Africa, I could then begin my re-entry back into the U.S. One of the first things that I had to get used to was the fact that everywhere I went there were White people. I kept wondering in my mind where are all the people of color were.

The next thing I noticed about being back home was that I had changed. My way of being and living had changed. Many of the biases that I had previously were gone. I was left with how I could explain this new way of thinking and feeling. I looked at people and saw them for who and what they are, beyond the color of their skin.

In my new role as interim minister for the Peoria Unitarian Church, I listened to the stories of those who were struggling for survival and for a chance to have an opportunity. I made a pact that I would do all that I could to stay engaged and to continue to listen and offer my help when it was requested.

I found myself in a very white congregation and a white community. I have not forgotten what I experienced in South Africa and strive in my daily interactions to teach love and acceptance of all. We all have a long way to go but I do know that we can love and support each other unconditionally, offering encouragement to those we encounter along our life's path journeys.

My partner and I are still not living in the same city, but we are fully committed to each other, and our relationship is strong. My illness helped us to realize that we never know just how much time any of us have. We are learning how to make the best of our current situation. We continue our practice of checking in with each other every day and celebrate this journey we are on.

As of this writing, the congregation in Cape Town is doing very well. A former Unity Minister, and a confirmed Buddhist, named Nina was hired to be their next interim minister. She is helping the members to celebrate their diversity and to find ways to engage with each other. Eventually, a fully trained Unitarian minister will be hired to continue to move the congregation forward. Thankfully, Nina is on board to help facilitate that process.

I will never forget my time spent in South Africa. It was an amazing experience and one that changed my life and gave me a greater appreciation for the opportunities that I have been able to take advantage of. I am a better person and a better minister because of serving the Cape Town Unitarian congregation. From the moment that my feet hit the ground to the moment that I left my life has been changed.

I have learned that no matter what language we speak, family background, or level of education, we typically have three things in common. We all want to feel a connection with ourselves and others. We all desire a sense of community where we can feel comfortable in our skin. And lastly, we all have a desire for a sense of purpose and that our lives matter.

My experience in South Africa helped me to identify many of my own biases and misunderstandings that I had regarding the cultures in Africa. In addition, I discovered what it means to embrace another's culture and to learn and grow from the people in that culture. Lastly, I have come to realize and understand just how small the world is and how we all are connected by the very nature of who we are.

CHAPTER TWELVE:
LESSONS I LEARNED

When I reflect upon my experience of living and working in South Africa, I am in awe of how this experience was life-changing for me. I am a Caucasian gay man who grew up in a white community and who had a very privileged upbringing. I say privileged not because of my family's socioeconomic status but privileged because I had opportunities available to me that my African American friends did not. I didn't have to worry about being stared at every time that I went into a store. I didn't have to worry I would be pulled over each time I saw a police car. I was free to walk and drive wherever I wanted to without fear of harassment.

I never realized what a privilege this was until I came face to face with the culture and people of South Africa. I have been blessed in my life with the opportunity to have many African American friends. They have been such a blessing in my life and have made me more compassionate and a better person. Yet until I experienced living in South Africa, I couldn't understand what their daily life was like living in America.

I still remember making that long walk through Cape Town Airport where international passengers make their way to customs. I knew instinctually that I was going to be in a country where I would be a minority, but then I came face to face with that reality. This was the first time in my life that I was the only white person. Growing up and coming out as gay at an early age, I was accustomed to being a minority in a crowd but usually, that difference didn't include the color of my skin.

Those feelings I felt the day I arrived in South Africa were very real for me. As the days and months rolled on, these feelings became less and less. I felt in some small way that wherever I went I was the minority. This provided me with a small understanding of what people of color must face here in America as they mingle and walk about. As I became more at ease with who I was and stopped making an issue that I was the only white person in the room, I learned to see people as they were and to meet them equally. This is a hard thing to describe or to put into words. For me, it was a gradual transformation; the color of my skin stopped being an issue whenever I entered a room, went to a restaurant, or took a ride on mass transit.

I quickly realized that I had many biases and that until I could debunk each one by taking it out and facing it, I couldn't get past my feeling of being uncomfortable. I felt what it is like to be a minority everywhere I went. I felt what I thought were stares and unuttered questions. This experience has provided me with a small understanding of just what people of color face each day in this country.

Learning how to serve the needs of a multi-cultural, multi-racial congregation was both challenging and a growth opportunity for me. One of the first things that I had to deal with was this idea by the members of the congregation that I was there to tell them what to do. They kept waiting for me to give them instructions and my instructions did not come. One day after a church service and before a leadership meeting, a member of the congregation asked me when I was going to tell them what to do.

My answer was simple, "I am not here to tell you what to do but to instead assist you in figuring it out. I will stand by your side and encourage you, but I will never dictate." There are multiple personalities in every Unitarian congregation where I have served, and Cape Town, South Africa was no different. The challenge any Minister has is how to motivate, encourage, and at times speak out. The best technique that I found to use was a simple one — I learned how to be quiet and just listen. From time-to-time different cultural norms arose, and different approaches to ways of thinking were displayed, but listening became the most widely used and effective tool.

South Africa is a land of many cultures, backgrounds, and ethnic diversity. Within the congregation and out of the church, South Africans have learned how to work with each other, survive, and get along. I found the members of the congregation to have that same kind of can-do spirit. This was evident one Saturday morning when many from the congregation showed up to help paint a school trailer in one of the coastal communities. A member of the church had contacted the nonprofit and had decided that we would paint the outside walls of this church.

This project took many hours and Saturdays to complete and many from the congregation participated. Another example was the annual pride celebration. A member took it upon herself to organize the celebration and to look for ways in which we could meet and work with other like-minded faith communities. We found those communities and together we all marched in the Pride parade.

I enjoyed learning about the various languages as well. I was teaching a class using Wayne B. Arnason and Kathleen Rolenz' book, "Worship That Works."[63]

I had eight people for a few weeks who met and gathered, and we discussed the topic of the arc of the service and the art of sermon writing. Over the

---

[63]Worship That Works: Theory and Practice for Unitarian Universalists, Second Edition KindleEdition by Kathleen Rolenz (Author), Wayne Arnason (Author), Nancy McDonald Ladd (Foreword)

next two months, each class member developed a sermon, wrote the sermon, and delivered it. It was amazing to watch and witness each of their unique growth processes.

I remember one class participant who shared that her first language was

Afrikaans and we encouraged her to write her sermon using her native tongue. She shared many of the words and what they meant in her language. It was a beautiful experience; I saw that day just how important language can be and how important it is to honor people's native language.

In ministry school, I learned about the concept referred to as the ministry of presence. I thought of it as always ensuring that as a minister you are present for whomever you are talking with. This is true, but in South Africa, I learned to go deeper into the ministry of presence. I learned it is listening to that which is not said verbally but communicated by way of the spirit and by actions and reactions is most important.

I found the South African people to be spiritual. They believe whole-heartedly in the holy spirit and that one can receive its guidance in all that one becomes engaged with. I learned from my members that the ministry of presence was taking in the whole and understanding what was being communicated nonverbally. I am thankful that the South African people furthered my understanding of the ministry of presence. I am a better listener and a more understanding minister because of it.

The South Africans taught me about listening to that inner voice. Their faith in a higher power is real. Under apartheid rule, so many of them could only hang onto their personal beliefs in a just and loving God. Things that we take for granted such as the right to choose where we live, walk, work and mingle were all taken from these people. They were told where they could walk, where they could work, and where they could congregate. It was their strong belief in a higher power that got most of them through the apartheid experience.

I saw and witnessed this faith. I remember a family that was struggling financially. They came to talk with me and ask for help. We worked with them and they held such a strong belief in a higher power that all I needed to do was be present and offer them counsel, support, and encouragement. They knew that the spirit would provide, and it did. Their simple act of faith was a testament to the strong power of belief.

So many times, as ministers we think we know the correct answer and so we formulate a response in our minds. In my interactions with the congregation, I had to be fully present and many times they were the ones to provide the answers, not me. I learned to listen fully and deeply to them. Sometimes listening was hard because of the language barrier. For many, English is the second language that they speak very well. Many of my congregants have such a thick accent that it was a challenge to hear and understand what they had to say.

Living in South Africa taught me the importance of self-care. Since I was the only ordained Unitarian Universalist minister on the whole continent of Africa, I found that my days off become ones of refueling my soul. I had to learn how to depend upon strength from within because I had no colleagues that I could visit with, no Unitarian national leadership that I could call up for a conversation, and my closest friend, my partner, was 8500 miles away.

My days off became ones of discovery and excitement. I used them to discover the many fun things to see and do in Cape Town. One day I went parasailing and on another, I went paragliding, and on another, bungee jumping. These and many more experiences helped to strengthen my soul. They provided me with the inner strength I needed to confront the challenges of living in a foreign country while providing ministry to a very mixed and varied congregation.

Much was required of me as a minister. Part of my challenge was to teach by example what the role of a minister was and just what a minister did on a day-to-day basis. Many members thought that all a Unitarian minister does is see the sick, and write and preach sermons on Sunday. I found that sharing my schedule with the congregation, helped them to understand many of the aspects of ministry. I am happy to report that at least three members of the Cape Town Congregation are now either enrolled in a seminary or taking the necessary steps to begin their seminary studies.

Many people in the USA have a different idea of what Africa is all about. The news media speaks of wars, civil disobedience, and strife. Yes, this does occur and is occurring in Africa. What I saw in South Africa was an awakening of the cultures. So much of Africa traces its roots back to the various tribes that they came from. With Colonialism and British, Dutch, and American Imperialism, many of these tribal traditions and cultures were lost. Because of Colonialism and Imperialism, Africa became a conquered continent. The conquerors told the natives what to do, how to worship, and who to worship. Many of the cultures in Africa are rising and are reclaiming their traditions and heritage. Throughout Africa, people are searching for a sense of community where they can be accepted for who and what they are. When new members came into my congregation in South Africa, they joined because they wanted a community and felt as if they had found it in Unitarian beliefs.

Africa is ready to take off and rediscover its unique identity and culture. Unitarian Universalism provides a good backdrop for this to occur. Many South Africans are rejecting the Christian faith that was forced upon them by their captives and their ancestors. They are searching for a place where they can connect as a community and a place where they can find love and support. I am excited about what is happening in South Africa and Africa in general. The best thing that all of us can offer is our unconditional support, friendship, and love.

Since being back in the United States, many have asked me, "What's next?" I have seen the good that can come from serving as a minister in a foreign country. There is a tremendous need for well-trained and vetted leaders. I also believe strongly that I now have the responsibility to share what I have learned with the congregations and others here in the USA. One thing that my life has taught me is to always keep my options open and be ready to accept whatever paths present themselves at the time. I will always cherish the time that I spent in South Africa. The people, the places, and the spirit of this country have changed my life for the better.

EPILOGUE

My memories of South Africa are still fresh in my mind. I have continued my work as a minister in the Unitarian Universalist faith. The lessons I learned, the skills I discovered, and the experiences I had in South Africa, are now a part of who I am. I look forward to making a trip back to South Africa and meeting and visiting with the people who shared and taught me so much.

My work with Unitarian Universalist congregations here in the United States has been both rewarding and challenging. Each experience in service has brought unique challenges and learning possibilities. I am thankful for the people of South Africa and their spirits, zest for life, and unique experiences that provided me with a foundation for my ministry.

Many of the elephants in my life have been exposed; to those things that I choose to not talk about. I have begun to deal with my bias and how I can live a life that is more understanding, less judgmental, and authentic. The people of South Africa taught me how to live that type of life. In those early morning hours when I sit and meditate, many times I can see the faces and the places of South Africa, and a smile comes to my face and a feeling of inner peace comes over me.

My commitment to life, service, and ministry has grown even more because of the experiences that I had in South Africa. I encourage each of you who read this book to think about what you can do to reach out to people who might be different than you but who could teach you a lot about how to live.

Cape Point View

Cape Point

Cape Town - Bantry Bay at Sundown

Cape Town City Center - Zulu Jazz Preformer

Cape Town City Center

Cape Town Schotsche Aloof (Bo Kemp)

Cape Town Unitarian Congregation

CapeTown Camps Bay

City of Cape Town

Company's Gardens Cape Town - Table Mountian

Flowers at Groot Constantia Winery

Front of the Unitarian Chrurch in Cape Town

Khayelitsha - Township- Non Profit Leaders

Market in Downtown South Africa

Kirstenbosch National Botanical Gardens

Kirstenbosch National Botanical Gardens 2

Native African Unitarian Ministers in Training

Newlands Southern Suburb of Cape Town - A South African Breakfast

Robin Island - Cape Town

Robin Island - The Walk of Freedom (Nelson Mandela)

Sea Poing - South Africa - My Place of Comfort

Sign at Zonnebloem - Cape Town

Table Mountain National Park

The Vinyards with Table Mountain

Unitarian US Choir performing with Our Cape Town Unitarian Choir

Wine Barrels

Zonnebloem - Cape Town

9 798885 906906